EARTH

MYSTERIES

THE
ELEMENT
LIBRARY

EARTH
MYSTERIES

PHILIP HESELTON

ELEMENT

Shaftesbury, Dorset

Rockport, Massachusetts

Brisbane, Queensland

© Element Books Limited 1995
Text © Philip Heselton

Published in Great Britain 1995 by
ELEMENT BOOKS LIMITED
SHAFTESBURY, DORSET SP7 8BP

Published in the USA in 1995 by
Element Inc.
PO Box 830, Rockport, MA 01966

Published in Australia in 1995 by
Element Books Limited for
Jacaranda Wiley Limited
33 Park Road, Milton, Brisbane, 4046

Designed and created by
THE BRIDGEWATER BOOK COMPANY
Art Director *Annie Moss*
Designer *Jane Lanaway*
Editor *Viv Croot*
Managing Editor *Anna Clarkson*
Picture Research *Vanessa Fletcher*
Page Make-up *Chris Lanaway*

Printed and bound in Italy by
Graphicom Srl

British Library Cataloguing-in-Publication Data available

Library of Congress Cataloging-in-Publication
Data available

ISBN 1–85230–714-5

❖

CONTENTS

INTRODUCTION

An Early Insight

Looking back on it, I can now see how many of the characteristics that were later to contribute to my interest in Earth Mysteries were present from an early age.

I liked to be alone walking in the Kentish woods, or cycling through the Surrey hills, or just being out at night on the nearest patch of open land looking at the stars.

It was most fortunate for me that the local library was well stocked with titles on astronomy, archaeology and geology, but it was the books on odd subjects such as flying saucers, psychic experiences, astrology and witchcraft that really caught my imagination and opened my eyes to new worlds. I will

ABOVE *A surviving example of an old straight track at Llanthony, Gwent, in Wales. The line passes through the Priory and straight up the hill beyond.*

always be grateful to that library.

Reading those books led indirectly to meeting Tony Wedd in 1961. He it was who first taught me about leys – alignments of ancient sites in the landscape, between which trackways are supposed to run, discovered by Alfred Watkins forty years previously.

It was Tony's enthusiasm that took hold of my mind. He strengthened my unorthodox side and encouraged me to take an active interest in leys for myself.

I followed where Watkins' 'old straight track' led, and I took others, including Jimmy Goddard, with me. He went further and faster along the track, and drew it to the

ABOVE *Use of the divining rod has long been a way of attuning to the earth spirit.*

attention of people such as John Michell who have been its champions. They discovered that it opened out into a whole network of interlinking paths: Earth Mysteries, as yet unnamed, was coming to life.

This coincided with the first appearance, in 1969, of photographs of the Earth as a ball of colour in the vastness of space, which reflected a very deep change of consciousness: we had become aware that life on Earth is one, and that what we do affects the whole.

At the same time, there was a corresponding exploration of inner space. Many were realizing that there were hidden dimensions to be explored which could no longer be brushed under the carpet as being psychic, esoteric or occult: they had become central to an understanding of life on Earth.

The combination of heightened ecological awareness with a more popular recognition of the reality of the psychic dimensions was the fertile bed from which Earth Mysteries emerged in the early 1970s. The name seems

to have been coined by a journalist in 1974, and it clearly found a niche, as if the time was right for coalescing of themes, attitudes and research activity into what Paul Devereux has called 'a multi-disciplinary and multi-mode Cauldron of Ceridwen'. Subjects and disciplines never before combined were drawn together, using both intuitive and analytical approaches.

Around the intial focus of leys, new insights and thoughts began to accumulate, and old ideas were thrown into a new perspective. Concepts such as earth energies began to be freely discussed; techniques such as dowsing were rediscovered or reinvigorated; legend and folklore were looked at in a new light and, above all, ancient sites were visited and the landscape seen with newly opened eyes.

Earth Mysteries was thus part of the growing tip of 'alternative' thinking and philosophy, challenging accepted ideas but at the same time offering a positive approach of its own.

RIGHT *When pictures of Earth were brought back from Apollo 17's historic voyage, they changed the way we saw our home and heralded a deep change of consciousness about our own planet.*

Because of the vital and pivotal nature of Earth Mysteries, it is perhaps inevitable that it attracts and has become the focus for what might be called modern mythology. From the old concept of 'Alfred Watkins astride his horse seeing the vision of glowing lines over the landscape' to the too easy acceptance of leys primarily as paths of energy which can readily be detected with a pair of dowsing rods, the myth is strangely attractive.

And yet, in order for Earth Mysteries to take its proper place as a major strand in the philosophy of the twenty-first century, we need to recognize the extent to which its study has matured over the last two decades. An exciting picture is emerging which, properly seen, is at least as attractive as the popular mythology of the subject.

I hope that this book will contribute to an understanding of the role of Earth Mysteries in the 1990s, as the subject grows towards maturity, continually expanding and redirecting its focus. Its rapidly changing character has made my task difficult but, by the same token, an important one at this time.

The origins of this book lie in a small booklet produced several years ago in response to the need for a concise introduction to Earth Mysteries.[80] The format of the series to which the present book belongs has enabled me to go into greater detail. While retaining the aim of providing an accessible guide which attempts to introduce the whole field, I hope that my approach will be sufficiently distinctive to enable the book also to interest those more 'grounded' in the subject.

Within the limits of the space available, I have tried to show how the often bewilderingly wide range of topics covered by the term Earth Mysteries has a unifying thread running through, weaving a web of interconnecting ideas and principles.

I have also aimed at producing a practical guide which will encourage readers to venture out into their local countryside and rediscover the old forgotten sacred sites.

BELOW LEFT *Fear of the unknown power of the earth, of the fairies carrying off a changeling, is giving way to understanding*

BELOW *Uluru (Ayers Rock), Australia , is a powerful centre of the earth spirit*

RIGHT *The pattern of the maze at Chartres cathedral, considered to be a powerful invocation of Earth energy.*

BELOW RIGHT *The Cheesewring, Bodmin Moor, Cornwall.*

As I hope will become clear in these pages, one of the princples of Earth Mysteries is that the earth is a living being – known to the Greeks as the goddess Gaia – and that we are a part of her. If we accept this, then we can relate to her in every part of the world. The underlying nature of Earth Mysteries is the same in the Australian desert as it is in the English countryside. I have tried to show this by using examples from all over the world, but there is a natural bias towards the places that I know best – England, and particularly East Yorkshire.

This book provides what I hope are useful clues, pointers and contacts. Our greatest teacher, however, must be the Earth herself, if we can allow ourselves to listen to her: I have endeavoured to show ways in which this can be done.

PHILIP HESELTON – *Hull, January 1995*

THE
LINEAR IMPULSE

*'I know now that in fully half a century's familiar contact with
this region my other self had, quite unknown to me, worked at one
subject ... The "Spirit of the British Countryside" ... had
surely been hovering near ...'*

The Old Straight Track, Alfred Watkins

ALFRED WATKINS AND THE DISCOVERY OF LEYS

Alfred Watkins was hardly the sort of person one would expect to start a movement which would radically affect the way in which we experience the landscape. In fact, he was the archetypal 'pillar of society': flour-miller, magistrate and county councillor.

Born in Hereford in 1855, he became known throughout his native county as he built up a detailed knowledge of the countryside of Herefordshire and the Welsh border. He was a pioneer photographer, inventing and selling the first popular exposure meter, and his natural empathy with the countryside is reflected in his photographs. He was also a prominent member of the Woolhope Naturalists Field Club, a well-respected society mainly devoted to the archaeology of Herefordshire.

Throughout his life several elements had been working within him: a deep knowledge and appreciation of the countryside, a sharp mind and a willingness to learn. On 30 June 1921 these elements coalesced and he suddenly saw that familiar landscape with new eyes. His son, Allen, recounts the discovery:

A chance visit to Blackwardine caused him to look at the map for features of interest. He had no particular object in mind, but was just having a look around. He noticed on the map a straight line that passed over hill tops through various points of interest and these points of interest were all ancient. Then without any warning it all happened suddenly. His mind was flooded with a rush of images forming one coherent plan. The scales fell from his eyes and he saw that over many long years of prehistory, all trackways were in straight lines marked out by experts on a sighting system. The whole plan of The Old Straight Track stood suddenly revealed.[132]

Watkins concluded that these straight trackways, which he came to believe had been known as 'leys', had 'landmarks' constructed along their route as a guide.

ABOVE *Alfred Watkins (1855-1935) was a pioneer photographer with a keen appreciation of the countryside.*

The Linked Chain
~

… imagine a fairy chain stretched from mountain peak to mountain peak, as far as the eye could reach, and paid out until it touched the 'high places' of the earth at a number of ridges, banks, and knowls. Then visualize a mound, circular earthwork, or clump of trees, planted on these high points, and in low points in the valley other mounds ringed round with water to be seen from a distance. Then great standing stones brought to mark the way at intervals, and on a bank leading up to a mountain ridge or down to a ford the track cut deep so as to form a guiding notch on the skyline as you come up. In a bwlch, or mountain pass, the road cut deeply at the highest place straight through the ridge to show as a notch afar off. Here and there and at two ends of the way, a beacon fire used to lay out the track. With ponds dug on the line, or streams banked up into 'flashes' to form reflecting points on the beacon track so that it might be checked when at least once a year the beacon was fired on the traditional day. All these works exactly on the sighting line. The wayfarer's instructions are still deeply rooted in the peasant mind to-day, when he tells you quite wrongly now – 'You just keep straight on'.

ALFRED WATKINS,
The Old Straight Track.

But could such tracks have survived, even as a remnant? Untold acres are being buried under bricks and mortar, and even in the countryside deep ploughing, ripping out of hedgerows and the widening of roads has seemingly obliterated most traces of the ancient landscape. There must have been a succession of road and track layouts over the years, so it would be fortunate indeed if even part of the original network had survived.

Watkins fully appreciated this and it is significant that his original 'vision' was of a series of markers stretched across the landscape rather than trackways as such. The idea of the continuity of sites over the generations is easier to accept for, if markers of some sort had been laid down, they might well have survived, even if their form had changed over time.

He started to plot lines of ancient sites and quickly got a feel for those which cropped up most frequently. He began to realize from the nature of these sites how the leys could have been constructed. It is actually a fairly simple matter, well within the capability of Neolithic and Bronze Age people, to set down a straight line across hilly country using three surveying poles. Watkins thought they were traders' tracks, laid out between terminal points, often hilltops, with intermediate waymarkers.

An example is the Saintbury ley, discovered by Devereux and Thomson.[35] It is 3½ miles (5.6km) long and runs from the heights of the Cotswolds down to the Vale of Evesham. The ley starts from a wayside cross next to a crossroads, goes through Saintbury Church, noted for its pagan survivals, through a Bronze Age round barrow, a Neolithic long barrow sited in the middle of an Iron Age fort, through a Saxon pagan cemetery, and an eighteenth-century beacon tower, ending at an ancient farmstead, Seven Wells – which was the subject of a fictional book on witchcraft by Hugh Ross Williamson, entitled *The Silver Bowl*.

A strange mixture! It is sometimes said that Watkins adopted such a variety of markers, including features of all types and ages, that his ideas can be discredited on this point alone. But, by understanding how he saw leys being constructed and operating, a picture begins to emerge of a system where each piece can be fitted into the whole.

ABOVE *The Long Man of Wilmington, cut into the South Downs in East Sussex, was thought by Watkins to be an illustration of the surveyors of the old straight track.*

RIGHT *Saintbury Church, Gloucestershire. the Saintbury ley passes straight through it.*

MARK POINTS

Terminal Points

Watkins believed that natural markers were used to set out the ley system. The most prominent of these were hilltops, and he found that all leys had a hilltop for at least one of their terminal points. While the highest hill in an area would often be used, it was more important that this should have a distinctive shape or be prominent in relation to the surrounding countryside.

Many of these hills have become known as holy and were often beacon sites. Watkins saw the origin of the beacon in the fires used to lay out the original alignments, and Tony Wedd used to quote Newman's hymn, 'Lead Kindly Light', as an unconscious memory of the process.

Other natural sites acting as terminal points are prominent rock outcrops, springs and holy wells. Watkins also considered that stone circles and henges could act as terminal points.

Waymarkers

Markers, the first of which were perhaps the surveying staffs themselves, were put in place to guide travellers. Joseph of Arimathea is reputed to have planted one at Wearyall Hill, which subsequently sprouted into the Glastonbury Thorn. Certainly thorn trees occur along leys, and planting is a way of establishing a mark with relatively little effort. Ideally, the marker trees would be of a species that was foreign to, or rare in, the area, and easy to distinguish by form and size at all seasons.

The Scots pine (*Pinus sylvestris*), which Watkins referred to as 'The Tree of the Ancient Track', meets several of these criteria. Although native to Scotland, it is evergreen, darker in appearance than most trees and tends to stand above the general canopy. Tony Wedd taught me to spot them as possible ley markers, and the sight of a clump or an individual pine standing alone on a ridge still fills me with excitement, perhaps a resonance with the ancient traveller to whom such a sight meant the security and guidance that the straight tracks provided.

Watkins admits that trees are 'a very weak point with the ley-hunter', meaning, of course, that, if leys are prehistoric, any existing trees could not possibly be original. They would have to be their descendants, by several generations.

It could happen. On the high points where the tree clumps are mostly situated, conditions may well be specially favourable for regenerated trees to survive to full maturity, thus helping to ensure the continuation of the position and form of the clump.

A further explanation can be found in the idea of 'tending' – that is, just as work is needed to keep a garden in good heart, so the clumps needed the active participation of local people to survive. Perhaps a nearby individual acted as 'guardian' of the site and did whatever was necessary: planting, fertilizing, weeding out weak specimens and keeping the clump within bounds. It seems at least possible that such a network of 'guardians' was still in place in Watkins' time. I have certainly heard of it happening in the present day, but the old methods are dying out as people become alienated from the countryside they live in.

Certainly many of the clumps are dying out. The impressive Cole's Tump, which Watkins photographed prominently silhouetted against the background of the Welsh mountains, may not survive the end of the century. This is verging on the tragic, because even if there is only a remote chance of these clumps being survivors from prehistoric times, it must be our duty to ensure their continuity.

ABOVE *Trees can be prominent landscape features, like this one at Place du Ris, Brittany, France, and may be the remnants of ancient mark-clumps.*

Cairns

In upland areas, significant markers could be made fairly easily with piles of stones. These 'cairns', as they are called, can reach enormous proportions, those on the tops of hills being capable in some instances of being seen for many miles.

Travellers might gradually have helped to make the marker more obvious. It seems to be a very deep-seated tradition, the need to add another stone to an existing pile, and many who climb hills today do so with a stone in their pocket to add a personal contribution to the cairn on the summit.

Markstones

Watkins also found much larger stones marking the leys, particularly in valleys. Typically, these are unworked and are chosen for their distinctiveness. In East Yorkshire they are glacial erratics, stones picked up in the last Ice Age, worn smooth, and deposited as the ice retreated. They are often rounded, but some have a flat top, which was often placed so that the sharpest edge or point indicated the direction of the ley. While they are heavy, it would have been quite possible, by co-operative effort, to move them into the right position to mark 'the line'.

Markstones can often be found on the roadside, in a bank or beneath a hedge. Winter is the best time to see them as they can get quite overgrown in summer. Watkins found them sited at intervals along a ley and often at the crossing of two leys.

Markstones can still be seen at road junctions and crossroads. A distinction needs to be drawn, however, with stones used to keep vehicles away from the corners of buildings. This is fairly easy in practice, although some markstones, because of their location, perform this function as well.

The stones may have been the origin of market sites, and have been the focus, or omphalos, around which market towns grew up. In Market Weighton, East Yorkshire, there is a markstone right in the middle of the town, opposite the church, and in Pembridge,

Herefordshire, Watkins found a markstone next to the market house.

Markstones are particularly vulnerable. Highway engineers' schemes for increasing the size of junctions often result in the stone being broken up for hardcore or being tossed unceremoniously aside. At best, it will be replaced by the new kerb, but its essential quality, its position, will have been lost.

They are also not usually recognized as having any significance by those responsible for statutory protection measures, particularly if they are suspected of having any connection with leys or other 'lunatic fringe' ideas. Fortunately, this is slowly changing. A new breed of archaeologist is emerging – more open-minded and willing to see signficance in the detail of the countryside which is slowly disappearing. Local residents, once given a hint, can be useful allies in preserving these forgotten features of their heritage.

BELOW *Cairns in the Black Mountains, Wales.*

RIGHT *Crossroads have
a special sanctity in
many traditions.*

Mounds

In time, more elaborate structures were built
on the lines, including mounds (or 'tumuli')
of earth and stone, 'burial chambers' and
dolmens or cromlechs. Natural high points
were emphasized by mounds, often slightly off
the hilltop, so that they could be seen from
the valley bottom. Watkins found many
mounds in this position on Radnor Forest.
They were never larger than was necessary for
them to be seen from the next point along the
line but were higher than the tops of any
forest trees in the vicinity.

Water

In low-lying land, the ditch which often
surrounded these mounds tended to fill with
water after rain, and Watkins saw a
progression to the circular moats which were
common in his district.

    Water is a key element in the ley system. It
seemed to Watkins to have a role both in
laying out the system and in guiding travellers.
Its signifance was in its reflecting qualities. If a
pond and beacon were both on the line, you
would only see the reflection of the beacon in
the pond if you were on the line too. More
generally, water will show up very well from a
distance by catching and reflecting light from
the sky.

    Ponds are the most obvious markers, and
we have the tradition, particularly on the
chalk downs and wolds, of 'dewponds',
constructed with layers of organic and
inorganic material to retain water even after a
prolonged dry spell.

    In some of the higher settlements the pond
is still the centre of the village; the church,
being more recent, is relegated to the edge.
Ashmore, in Cranborne Chase, is a classic
example, and there are many similar villages
in the Yorkshire Wolds. Leys can often be
found passing through the pond and the
church in a village and it is always worth
trying this out where the pond seems ancient.

    Fords and bridge sites often change little
over the years and Watkins cites several
examples of leys crossing rivers at fords.

Camps

Hilltop earthworks, somewhat misleadingly
called 'camps' or 'hill forts', are often found
to have their form determined by leys, the
straight sections of embankment being aligned
on distant markers. Watkins found that the
earthworks around Hereford, such as Dinedor
and Capler, followed this pattern.

Roads and Tracks

Today we are seeing a system in decay, but
surprisingly often we find stretches of road
and track coinciding with the old alignments.

    Watkins found crossroads falling on leys
with amazing frequency, even though the
present-day roads were not aligned on the
leys. It was the site which had remained
unchanged. Crossroads have a special place in
tradition. Witches were supposed to meet
there. Certainly those who had been accused
of witchcraft or committed suicide could not
be buried in the churchyard: second best was
usually the crossroads, a memory perhaps of
some measure of sanctity which may over
time have become attached to leys because of
their association with other sacred sites.

Evidence of trackways can still sometimes be found. Watkins particularly noted notches where the ley went over a hilltop. These were valuable indicators, as they would only show up from a distance if you were 'on the line'.

Churches

Watkins' inclusion of churches as mark points is particularly controversial: these dated from Saxon times at the earliest, whereas leys were claimed to be prehistoric.

This objection could be countered by examples of churches known to have been built on pagan sites, such as Cascob, Radnorshire and Fimber, East Yorkshire, which were actually built on tumuli. Also in East Yorkshire are Goodmanham, which was built on the site of a pagan temple, and Rudston, where the church is adjacent to the tallest standing stone in Britain. The process was set out clearly in a letter from Pope Gregory to Bishop Mellitus in CE601:

ABOVE Pagan survivals are now being increasingly recognized. This 'Green Man' on the façade of Worms Cathedral, Germany, although carved in the nineteenth century, replaces a much earlier image.

I have come to the conclusion that the temples of the idols in England should not on any account be destroyed. Augustine must smash the idols, but the temples themselves should be sprinkled with holy water and altars set up in them in which relics are to be enclosed… I hope the people (seeing their temples are not destroyed) will leave their idolatry and yet continue to frequent the places as formerly, so coming to know and revere the true God.

BELOW The pre-Christian altar at Saintbury Church stands as witness to the pagan history of this site.

So the Church took over the sites (and in some cases the very buildings) where the pagan gods and goddesses were worshipped. This process of Christianization was slow: the people clung to their pagan beliefs, and saw no difficulty in combining the two faiths. The study of pagan survivals in English churches is fascinating, and writers such as Guy Ragland Phillips have shown that churches are still full of pagan symbolism.[108]

Churchyard and wayside crosses are often the result of a similar process. Standing stones, particularly in Devon and Cornwall, were Christianized with a carved cross and cross bases were made from large stones, like markstones, with sockets cut into their tops.

Site Continuity

Even if they were first established in prehistoric times, knowledge use and even construction of leys may have continued well into the medieval period, perhaps as the secret inheritance of certain esoteric orders.

Particularly in the older towns and cities such as London, Bristol and Cambridge, there is evidence that churches were built on leys. Brian Larkman has discovered what he calls the 'Corridor of Sanctity' in York, leading from the confluence of the Rivers Ouse and Foss, through the site of a Templar chapel, the massive Clifford's Tower, and five other medieval churches, including the Minster.[78]

Certainly, the mark points survived while the old straight tracks fell into disuse and neglect. New structures often replaced the old on the same site. As well as churches, Watkins quotes numerous examples of 'castle mounds' which developed from earlier structures.

Surprisingly frequently, leys also pass exactly through important and isolated farmsteads often on a similar orientation to the main buildings. There is a ley which runs east from the Yorkshire village of Sproatley to the coast. It goes through four churches, a stone and a moat, as well as being followed by a road for much of its length. In the village of Humbleton, as well as passing through the church, the ley runs through the two major farmsteads in the village.

Place names

Place names may provide a clue when the physical marks have gone. As an example, Tony Wedd quotes One Tree Hill where a ley crosses the Greensand Ridge in Kent. The hilltop is now completely wooded over, but the name remains as witness to a possible mark.[134]

Place names change over the years, in some cases quite substantially, and Watkins warned against too easy an acceptance of a name at face value. The most obvious is the word 'ley'. Whilst he considered that the old straight tracks had actually been called 'leys', Watkins did not disagree with the orthodox interpretation of this element as 'pasture' or 'field'. However, he thought that this meaning had evolved from the original word for a straight track, via the clearing of the woodland through which it passed, to the more common present-day meaning. He quotes examples, such as Ley Rock, near Tintagel, and Bonsall Leys, high up on the Derbyshire moors, to demonstrate that the word did not always refer to pasture.

Watkins also gives meanings for the obsolete word 'leye' as, firstly, an island, and secondly, flame, blaze or fire, both, as we have seen, relating to the laying out of the old straight track. He considered that the expression 'the lay of the land' was an unconscious memory of the original use of the word. There is also confirmation in the word 'laia', meaning 'a roadway in a wood', and the French words *layon* meaning a track used by sportsmen, and *laie* meaning a bridleway or forest ride.[105]

Watkins ceased to use the word 'ley' towards the end of his life, and caution should be exercised in using the element as evidence of an old straight track.

In his researches, Watkins found the elements 'cole', 'dod', 'red', 'white' and 'black' indicative of a trackway. He thought 'cole' and 'black' referred to charcoal and to its use for the marker beacons. 'Red' and 'white' referred to traders' tracks specializing in pottery and salt respectively. 'Dod', he speculated, could have been the name for the original surveyors, 'dodging' about.

THE QUEST FOR LEYS: HOW TO FIND THEM

How do we go about finding leys? We don't all have Watkins' advantages: a lifetime's familiarity and sympathy with his native countryside; the photographer's eye for detail, for the unusual and for the properly framed view; and the advantage of access to the countryside as part of his daily work.

We must start from where we are, as urbanized humanity. Even if we live in the countryside, we are likely to be alienated from the land and so must create the link afresh. For this we need the three resources of mapwork, fieldwork and archive work, blended with intuition.

Reading the map

Ordnance Survey maps are essential: they are accurate and of good quality. The 1:50,000 series is the most useful scale to start with. Any likely leys can then be checked on the 1:25,000 maps. Get flat maps for preference as folds can distort the line somewhat.

For the most detail, the first editions of the old 6-inch maps are invaluable. These can probably be consulted at your nearest local history library. The newer 1:10,000 maps don't have nearly as much detail. This is partly due to a real loss of features in the countryside as a result of modern agricultural practices, and party due to the present policy of the Ordnance Survey.

So, get the local sheet of the 1:50,000 Ordnance Survey and lay it out on the table. Think about the mark points that are most likely to be indicated on the map: village churches, tumuli and 'castle mounds', stone circles and standing stones, wayside crosses and beacon sites.

Just play around with the map for a while, together with a sharp pencil and a long transparent ruler. Let intuition take over and see whether you can find some promising lines, passing through several of these points. If you find a likely line, see if there is confirmation by way of stretches of road following the line, road junctions, crossroads

or fords falling on it, or some of the place name elements Watkins referred to. You will probably get some sort of feeling when you are 'on the right track'.

This is only the start, however, as many potential mark points won't appear on the map: at some stage you have to follow up with fieldwork. A ley can really only be said to be confirmed if it has been walked for most of its length.

Walking the track

Sometimes following the track you have mapped is not possible, as care has to be taken to keep to public footpaths or ask landowners' permission. For those with motor transport, a possible procedure is to follow the line as closely as possible by public roads, stopping where the line crosses to observe and explore.

In particular, the high and low points on the line should be noted and investigated for possible sighting markers. Draw a cross-section along the line by noting where the contours cross and gradually build up a profile of the ley on a separate piece of paper. The visibility of one point from another can then be determined and the likely sighting spots found. Tony Wedd gave the example of an alignment of Scots pine clumps in Kent between Lyewood Common and Kent Hatch. There were four clumps accurately aligned, and each was on a high point on the line, sited for maximum visibility.[68]

In fieldwork, you are really looking for anything that might confirm the existence of a ley. Markstones buried in a hedge bottom or by the side of the road, tree clumps on prominent sites that can be seen from a distance, earthworks that might be indicative of an old sunken way, or indeed anything unusual on the line. It is surprising how often field gates, for exampole, are exactly on a ley.

Local residents can be helpful, as Allen Watkins found on his first ley walk. Unprompted, a farm labourer told him of the tradition of an old track precisely on the line where he had surmised the ley to be.[130]

You will quickly pick up the 'feel' of a ley and know when you are exactly on it. This may be something intuitive, but it is also a matter of visual 'rightness'. Watkins always said that the best photographs are taken 'along the ley'. Certainly a picture often seems to be 'framed' perfectly in such cases. Incidentally, it is a good idea to take photographs where possible as sites are still disappearing at a rapid rate.

Winter is a good time for fieldwork. Not only will markstones show up more easily when undergrowth has died down, but earthworks can be seen more readily in the low-angle winter sun.

Researching the archives

There are many clues hidden amongst the archives of the local library or museum. The old Victorian antiquarians often observed much that would nowadays be ignored. The Transactions of the local Archaeological, Antiquarian or Historical Society, or specialist local histories, often refer to features in the landscape such as stones or holy wells which have since vanished or been forgotten about. There may be folklore or legends attached to sites, which should always be recorded. The County Sites and Monuments Records, now likely to be on computer, give details of all archaeological sites. Aerial photographs can be another valuable source of information.

When you have researched a ley, by map, field and archive, you are then in a position to write up the material for possible publication in a magazine such as *The Ley Hunter*. Articles on well-documented leys are usually welcomed.

In time, you will begin to build up quite a body of knowledge on the ley system in your area, and may start to host trips for your local Earth Mysteries group. Certainly, at the very least, the quest for leys adds interest to visits to the countryside.

BELOW *Features on leys can often show up most clearly in the winter landscape, when vegetation and sun are both low*

2

A
LIVING TRADITION

'*T he subject touches a deep nerve in the modern mind, precisely
because of its archetypal nature. The straight line in the landscape,
the result of another kind of human awareness interacting with a differently-
perceived environment, reminds us that we have forgotten certain things. We
have forgotten about our inner life; we have forgotten that the land is sacred,
and we have forgotten the interaction between them both*'

Lines on the Landscape, Nigel Pennick and Paul Devereux

STRAIGHT TRACKS AROUND THE WORLD

ABOVE *The presence of linear landscape features, such as here at Nasca, Peru, is now recognized as a world-wide phenomenon.*

What I have called the 'linear impulse' seems to be found in widely distant parts of the world. Paul Devereux has called it 'a primary experience', something deeply seated in the human psyche.

This was not the opinion of the archaeologists who attacked Watkins' ideas following publication of *The Old Straight Track* in 1925. O.G.S. Crawford refused a paid advertisement for the book in the journal *Antiquity*, his objection centring around the view that prehistoric people did not walk in straight lines, as all the undoubted prehistoric roads were winding.

Such criticism was premature, as it is now clear that in many parts of the world long, dead-straight trackways were laid out and, in several cases, are still used.

Watkins knew of the Chin tracks in India which follow the most direct line between villages regardless of gradient; the straight camel tracks of Palestine, sighted on tree clumps on ridges, notched where the line went through; and the skyline cairns of Egypt set up as landmarks for caravans. He quotes from Johnston's *Uganda*:

The broad native roads made as straight as possible for their mark, like the roads of the Romans, seem to pick out preferentially the highest and steepest hills, which they ascend perpendicularly and without compromise.[128]

It is in the American continent, however, that the most complete evidence is to be found. Watkins wrote of the Cree Indian tracks always being straight, and recent findings in Chaco Canyon, New Mexico, confirm the existence of long straight tracks laid down by the Anasazi.[105]

Though not tracks as such, the lines of Nasca, in Peru, are strikingly similar. They were first noticed in 1926, but only following aerial photography in the 1930s was their extent recognized. Situated on a plateau between the coast and the mountains, straight lines, geometrical figures, trapezoids and shapes of animals are outlined on the desert surface – they seem to have been made by scraping away the darker top layer of sand to reveal a lighter layer underneath. Lack of rainfall means that these intriguing patterns have survived intact for hundreds of years, though they are now being threatened by tourists.

Higher up in the mountains is the system of *ceques* centred on the old Inca capital of Cuzco. Radiating out from the Temple of the Sun, where the Inca presided, were the *ceques*, or alignments of shrine sites known as *huacas*. Many are stones or springs, others bridges or gullies. Some have been Christianized, others destroyed or their use changed. Enough of these *huacas* remain, however, for the biologist Tony Morrison to have plotted several *ceques* and recorded them by infra-red photography as narrow lines in the vegetation.

Morrison found more evidence of the linear impulse in Bolivia. Straight tracks up to 50 miles (80 km) in length, often aligned to a mountain top, were still in use by local inhabitants. They were marked by piles of stones, particularly at intersections, and churches were frequently found on them. Sacrifices and offerings are still made at sites along the lines, and festivals take place on them. Morrison's aerial photographs show narrow paths going straight across miles of rugged countryside.[97]

A QUESTION OF PROOF

ABOVE *The Devil's Arrows, Boroughbridge, Yorkshire. Alignments from these standing stones have now been statistically proved.*

On the face of it, leys are ideally suited to a statistical approach. You have a number of points on a map: some are aligned. What is the likelihood that such alignments would occur through chance alone?

Yet, as we look closer the difficulties multiply. The essence of the problem is to define a ley, which is harder than it appears. What markers are we going to accept, for example, and how can we define them with precision? Do we have enough information over, say, a single map sheet to be able to plot all the potential ley markers including those that are not on the map? How accurately do the points have to be aligned before we accept them as a ley? None of these questions yet has a satisfactory answer.

Watkins himself was the first to attempt some sort of statistical assessment. He took the One inch to One mile Ordnance Survey sheet for the Andover area, noting that there were fifty-one churches on the map. Plotting alignments, he found eight cases of four churches aligning and one example of a five-church line. As a comparison, he took a similar-sized piece of paper and marked 51 crosses at random. He found only one instance of four points aligning and none of five. The number of three-point alignments was much the same in each case. His conclusion was that four-point alignment was strong evidence of design rather than accident.[128]

This is essentially what more recent statisticians are trying to do: to compare actual alignments with those obtained by random methods. The difficulty was always to obtain sufficiently high-quality data within a defined area. In 1974, John Michell produced a detailed study of alignments in West Penwith, Cornwall, supported by extensive fieldwork.[92] It is the best area in Britain for megalithic sites, and is surrounded on three sides by the sea.

Michell's work provided the opportunity researchers had been waiting for and Pat Gadsby and Chris Hutton-Squire, of the alternative technology magazine, *Undercurrents*, took up the challenge.

For the first time, a computer was used in the analysis. The positions of the fifty-three sites mentioned by Michell were plotted. Alignments between these points were found by computer. Random number tables were then used to generate a set of fifty-three imaginary references. Each point was 'nudged' randomly within its own grid square, so that the overall clustering was retained but any alignments destroyed. The analysis was then repeated with the simulated data.

The results of the computer run using the real sites showed a five-point alignment, which would be expected by chance only once in 250 runs. There were also five four-point alignments, where less than one would be expected. The odds against getting the 51 three-point alignments obtained are 160 to 1. The study has been criticized for incompleteness of data, but it was a major step forward, and the results obtained were so positive that further research was stimulated.[51]

Robert Forrest and Michael Behrend are currently in the forefront of statistical ley research.[46] They have gradually refined their techniques over the years, with additional factors, such as ley length, continually being built in to the equation. The best leys, such as the alignment of the Devil's Arrows standing stones in Yorkshire with the Thornborough Henges, pass their tests well, but the statistical models used are still not entirely adequate to cope fully with the real distribution of sites in the landscape.

THE IDEAS EMERGE

There can, however, be no doubt about the way in which Watkins' discovery caught the public imagination.

Certainly he was not the first to have been struck by the idea, and in his first book on leys he quotes a reference from 1882 in which G.H. Piper notes an alignment of several sites in Herefordshire.[127]

In 1870, when Watkins was 15 years old, the British Archaeological Association held its annual Congress in his native Hereford. One of the speakers was William Henry Black, a historiographer at the Public Record Office in London. He had been working since the 1820s on his theory that 'grand geometrical lines' had been laid out in ancient times across the country and that these were indicated by old boundaries and markers.[7]

Archive investigations by Nigel Pennick and others have revealed numerous examples from Victorian times onwards of work on the alignment of ancient sites. One of the earliest was the Reverend Edward Duke who, in the 1840s, found that several prehistoric sites, including Avebury, Silbury Hill and Stonehenge were aligned north-south with each other. He went further and tied the distances between the sites in with the known distances between planets in the solar system.[41]

By the turn of the century, alignment research was on the increase, although it was being carried on by individuals working in isolation from each other. C.W. Dymond was plotting alignments at the Stanton Drew stone circle in Somerset. As early as 1889, Joseph Houghton Spencer plotted lines through churches, barrows, beacon sites and fragments of path, considering them to be remnants of a system of ancient signal stations. And Francis J. Bennett was investigating a parallel system of meridional (north-south) lines in Kent, on which both megalithic sites and churches fell.[103]

Following extensive researches into the orientation of Egyptian temples, the eminent astronomer, Norman Lockyer, turned his attention in 1901 to Stonehenge. He extended the midsummer sunrise line in both directions to pass through the top of Sidbury Hill to the north-east, and touch the earthworks of Grovely Castle and Castle Ditches in the other direction. He also found an alignment, discovered independently by Watkins, linking Stonehenge, Old Sarum (the old site of Salisbury), Salisbury Cathedral and Clearbury Ring earthworks.[83]

Lockyer's ideas were taken up in Germany by researchers such as Albrecht and Leugering, the latter of whom, in the 1920s, found alignments in his native Westphalia. He was helped by Josef Heinsch, who found further alignments, particularly some oriented six degrees north or south of due east, which he called a 'solar year line', linking a 'holy hill' in the west, dedicated to the moon, with a solar site in the east.

Germany in the 1920s and 30s was fertile ground for such ideas. Any work which demonstrated ancient Germanic culture was seized upon and given official patronage. A notable beneficiary of this was Wilhelm Teudt (1860-1942). Independently of Albrecht and Heinsch, he found a network of 'holy lines' oriented on astronomical phenomena. Along these lines were beacons and 'watchtowers', and he found that from any earthwork there would be an orientation marker in the form of a 'watchtower' along north-south or east-west axes.[94]

BELOW The significance of the placing of Silbury Hill, Wiltshire, the largest artificial mound in Europe, in its surrounding landscape has long been recognized.

THE STRAIGHT TRACK CLUB

It was through Watkins that interest and ideas about the linear impulse burgeoned. Following his initial vision, Watkins worked quickly and with enthusiasm, fuelled by the stored experience of over fifty years. As he put it:

><><

> ... half the year had gone, the clear smoke-free distances of early summer a thing of the past, and midsummer day over, before I got the first clue. Once started, I found no halt in the sequence of new facts revealed by active search on the tracks.[127]

><><

He gave a lecture to the Woolhope Club in September 1921 illustrated with his own lantern slides. There was encouragement for the lecture to be published, and the following year an edited transcript appeared, accompanied by selected photographs.[127]

Meanwhile, Watkins continued his researches with increased vigour, and three years later, in 1925, his magnum opus, *The Old Straight Track*, was published.[128] Readers started to send him examples of leys in their own districts and, as a result of their enthusiasm, the Straight Track Club was formed in 1926. Members corresponded by means of postal portfolios, whereby papers were circulated, each member adding their own contribution as the package went round. The club had field meetings, following leys and visiting ancient sites, a member who knew the area acting as leader. Members came from a variety of backgrounds, many as knowledgeable about their own regions as Watkins was about his.

The portfolios are now in Hereford Central Library. They include several volumes of maps, photographs, accounts of leys, theories and confirmation from various sources. They reveal the lively interchange of ideas that took place, including the expansion and development of Watkins' original work.

Major F.C. Tyler, a leading member of the club, was instrumental in this. He had become increasingly unhappy about the trackway theory, feeling it to be insufficient

to account for the number of leys which seemed to exist, the tendency for parallel systems, the intersection of many leys at a single site, and the phenomenon which he discovered of patterns of concentric circles. Tyler felt that the only explanation was that the sites were all points in some widespread pattern, that there was a sanctity to the sites and that this was the reason that they were marked in ancient times. His book, *The Geometrical Arrangement of Ancient Sites*, appeared in 1939.[125]

In the 1930s, Donald Maxwell produced a series of guide books[90] which introduced ley-hunting to a much wider audience until it became, in the words of *The Birmingham Post*, 'a new outdoor hobby'.

The Straight Track Club was wound up in 1948, but ideas were kept alive through Egerton Sykes' Avalon Society. He published a paper by ex-sapper Kenneth Koop, in which a case is made for the alignments being the remains of an early survey of Britain.[75]

Current interest in leys really dates from 1961, when ex-RAF pilot Tony Wedd, published a small booklet entitled *Skyways and Landmarks*, which postulated a link between UFO sightings and mark points on the ground.[134]

I met him one spring day 30 years ago in the beautiful Kentish countryside where he lived. He was a free-thinker – one whose thoughts ranged widely over every unorthodox idea, forging connections where none had previously been contemplated.[67]

From him, I heard of leys for the first time, and learned that he had found alignments of tree clumps in the countryside around his home.

I was fired with his enthusiasm and on my reluctant return home ordered *The Old Straight Track* from the library. From this, I learned more about leys and immediately got out the local map to try and find one for myself. I succeeded almost immediately and found a good alignment of moats ending at Gill's Lap pine clump on Ashdown Forest, one of the marks noted by Tony Wedd.

ABOVE *Mark Beech, Kent A reported UFO sighting here inspired researchers to connect the trees to mark points on the ground.*

A schoolfriend, Jimmy Goddard, was similarly inspired and together we formed The Ley Hunters Club. With the help of Tony Wedd and Egerton Sykes I tried to contact surviving members of the Straight Track Club. Many of my envelopes came back 'Return to Sender', and it was clear that most members had died or were very elderly. Several did respond, however, and I fondly remember visiting such people as Joan Hatton, Christine Crosland-Symms, Charles Mayo and Harold Fletcher Trew in their own homes. They were all very heartened that someone was at last taking an interest: I only wish I had had a tape recorder!

Allen Watkins agreed to be President of the club and spoke at its inaugural meeting in November 1962 (the same day as the founding of the Findhorn Community in Scotland, such are the synchronicities of the universe!). He talked of his father's psychic abilities and also of the way in which Alfred Watkins had come to see the ley mark points in terms of the old elements: fire, earth, air and water. He believed that they could so perfectly fit this classification that one of the functions of leys was for ritual or teaching purposes.[131]

We started a small newsletter to which, in 1965, we gave the title *The Ley Hunter*: it is still flourishing, over 30 years later. Jimmy gave a series of talks, including one which was attended by John Michell and Paul Devereux. He started their interest in the subject and they have since become prominent in the field. Many others were brought into the subject during the 1960s, including Anthony Roberts, Nigel Pennick and Paul Screeton.

The subject also expanded greatly in scope from that of the study of leys, and one theme which began to be explored was that of folklore. A wealth of legends and folk tales has been recorded, much of which relates to particular sites in the countryside. What excited many of those who were following leys was the realization that the legends were about the very same sites which Watkins had found to be ley markers. This line of inquiry proved to be a rewarding path which was, however, to lead in a most unexpected direction.

BELOW *Ashdown Forest, Sussex, the site of pioneering work on tree clump alignments.*

RIGHT *Mont St Michel, Normandy, France, has been a natural focus for legends and folk tales since remote antiquity.*

3

FOLKLORE
AND
LANDSCAPE

Only in the last hundred years have most people in the developed world been able to read and write. Before that time, knowledge and wisdom were passed on through the spoken word, as they still are in much of the world. This is the essence of folklore, much of which consists of stories and legends about sites, both natural and artificial, in the countryside.

ABOVE *Arthur's Stone at Cefn Bryn, Glamorgan, Wales. There are many sites all over Britain and northern France that claim a relationship with the mythical king.*

The eighteenth-century antiquarians started to collect tales they heard. Oral tradition was written down and gained a wider currency than ever before. Publication was stimulated by the late-nineteenth and early twentieth-century revival of interest in folk customs, and accounts from many places throughout the British Isles and beyond are to be found in published collections, often by county.

They show an enormous variety within which certain common themes can be noticed.

Many legends are attached to natural features in the landscape, such as prominent hills, rocks and springs; others to some of the most ancient surviving artificial structures such as standing stones, stone circles and barrows, churches and wayside crosses. The parallel with Watkins' mark points was too striking to ignore, and attracted attention from those who felt that folklore might provide a clue to understanding leys.

But, what is folklore? Is it just a collection of stories or does it contain memories of real experiences? And how old is it? Some may be relatively recent, like urban belief tales, but others are much more ancient, altered so that we no longer have any idea of their origin.

The point about folklore is that it has to be interpreted. The tales must have changed significantly over the generations. Allen Watkins used to say that there was a core of truth hidden in the heart of all folk tales and

ABOVE *The enigmatic Pied Piper, a figure from folklore, who lured the children of Hamelin to a mysterious mound which opened up to swallow them all.*

legends if we can only find it amongst the accumulations which have occurred over time: the difficulty arose in finding out what it was – of winnowing the wheat from the chaff.

One of the principles underlying Earth Mysteries is that unusual things do happen at certain places in the countryside. Folklore can be seen, at least in part, as the distorted memory of such events and experiences. These are still occurring and, ultimately, there is no clear distinction between folk tales of unknown origin and accounts of events which have taken place within living memory. Any difference is one of degree rather than kind.

In the 1970s there was a renewed interest in site-related folklore in Britain. Two books, *Folklore of Prehistoric Sites in Britain* by Leslie Grinsell[59] and *The Secret Country* by Janet and Colin Bord[11], appeared in 1976 and have been essential in preparing this chapter. Of course similar themes occur in other parts of the world.

LIVING STONES AND OTHER SITES

Of all the types of site which have folklore attached to them, stones, both natural outcrops and deliberately placed structures, are pre-eminent. The legends are consistent in widely separate places and give a good cross-section of the main themes.

So, what legendary properties did the stones possess? A surprising number have tales which suggest some form of 'activity', almost as if they were alive. This seems a strange notion at first glance, as stones are the archetype of solid, unmoving form, the very symbol of permanence and immutability.

ABOVE *Men-an-Tol, Cornwall, has reputed healing properties.*

While their names apparently have other origins, the Tingle Stone and the Twizzle Stone, both in Gloucestershire, are very suggestive of just the sort of effects which have been reported at standing stones in recent years. The first time I visited the Hart Stone in County Durham with Paul Screeton in 1969, for example, I experienced strong tingling and Paul has recounted cases where the stone appeared to have healing properties.[114] There is also a whole group of stones, of which Grinsell[59] notes 39, which involve the movement of stones.

MOVING STONES

ABOVE *The Wergin
Stone, near Hereford,
moved mysteriously
by night and so heavy
that it had to be
dragged back to its
place by oxen.*

A common belief was the impossibility of counting the stones of a stone circle. The Countless Stones at Aylesford in Kent are the remains of a chambered tomb: a baker is said to have tried to solve the problem by placing a loaf on each stone, but the Devil kept knocking them off. The same legend may have attached itself to tree clumps as well. A.A. Milne refers to the clump at Gills Lap (which he called Galleons Lap) as being enchanted because no one had been able to count the number of trees, even by tying string round each trunk as it was counted.[95]

As mentioned above, stones traditionally have healing properties. The Cornish holed stone, Men-an-Tol, is reputed to cure a variety of afflictions, particularly of a rheumatic nature. Children with rickets were passed naked through the hole three times and then drawn along the grass three times in an easterly direction. Adults had to crawl nine times through the hole against the sun.

Physical contact was often thought necessary. Canna's Stone at Llangan in Carmarthenshire was said to cure ague. The sufferer was to sit, and preferably sleep, on the stone after partaking of the waters from a nearby well.

I first heard of the phenomenon of moving stones when camping at the foot of Bredon Hill in Worcestershire in 1960. At the very top of the hill is a natural outcrop known as the Banbury Stone. Local legend states that when it hears the church clock strike 12 it goes down to the River Avon to drink. This is but one variation on a theme – other legends state that the relevant time is midnight, cock crow, sunrise or noon. Some specify particular times of year, such as New Year, Easter Sunday morning, Midsummer, or All Hallows Eve. The stones are sometimes said to turn round or dance before going down to the local stream or lake to drink. Natural outcrops, standing stones and stone circles are all involved in the activity.

According to legend, some stones have moved permanently by their own power, such as the Wergin Stone near Hereford which suddenly moved 240 paces and required nine yoke of oxen to take it back. Others, such as the Hoar Stone at Enstone, Oxfordshire, will go back to their original position if moved. The Blaxhall Stone in Suffolk is reputed to have grown from the size of a loaf to a block of five tons in a century, and Drewton Pillar in East Yorkshire was believed to grow again when fragments fell from it.

Along with healing, stones were thought to bestow fertility. The Tolven Stone in Cornwall assured fertility in a person if he or she crawled naked through the hole in it. Other stones would ensure an engagement, the success of a marriage, or the easing of childbirth. Women who desired children would visit the King Stone, Warwickshire, at full moon and rub their breasts on its surface.

A tale which seems linked with fertility is that of the White Cow of Mitchell's Fold, a stone circle in Shropshire. A white cow used to provide milk for everyone in the locality, but it was customary for only one pailful to be taken. There arrived 'one of evil life', who milked the cow into a sieve, until it was milked dry. The cow disappeared and never returned, and the evil one was turned into the tallest stone in the circle.

The Tale of the Glowing Stone

~

About half way down the hill forming the eastern slope of Nafferton Slack [in Yorkshire], by the road-side, to prevent waggons leaving the roadway, stood a large stone, which was believed to have wonderful powers. At night, at certain seasons, it glowed like fire, sometimes it seemed but the portal of a well-lighted hall; and one old stone-breaker declared he had heard wonderful music issuing therefrom, the like of which he had never heard before; while on one occasion he had seen troops of gaily-dressed elfins repairing thither, some on foot and some in carriages, and they all went into this mysterious hall.[89]

There is a strong tradition that it is bad luck to disturb a standing stone or stone circle and fear of retribution has undoubtedly helped preserve many that might otherwise have been removed for building stone, gateposts and the like. Illness or disease could result from ignoring such strictures and cattle could become ill if stones from an ancient site were incorporated into the walls of their shelter.

The sudden onset of severe weather conditions was thought to be a frequent result of disturbance to a site. At Burley Camp in Devon a crock of gold is said to be buried, but anyone who tries to dig for it is said to be scared away by thunder and lightning. Lewis Edwards tells of someone who wanted to break up the Hobgoblin Stone (Carreg-y-Bucci) in Wales for gateposts. He was told: 'No sooner had I got out my tools than there was a violent thunderstorm, the worst I have ever known. I ran for my life, but it followed me all the way home.'[42]

More positively, veneration was shown by leaving offerings. At midnight on a full moon maidens used to leave cakes or barley-meal, honey and milk on Arthur's Stone, Gower. They then crawled round the stone three times on hands and knees, hoping to see their future sweethearts.

The tradition that stone circles and standing stones are human beings who have been turned to stone because of some misdemeanour is widespread and seems to point to some memory of the ritual use of

these sites in ancient times. Grinsell notes this tradition associated with more than a dozen stone circles from Cornwall to Scotland. Chris Castle notes that a stone circle in the Senegambian area of West Africa is popularly supposed to be a bridal party turned to stone.[16]

The actions responsible for this misfortune vary from dancing on the Sabbath, dancing through the night until sunrise, refusing to accept Christianity, and peering uninvited at festivities. The stones at the Merry Maidens stone circle in Cornwall are said to be musicians who accelerated their pace until they became petrified with exhaustion.

It is interesting that certain numbers seem to occur frequently in folklore, particularly three, seven and nine. There are several circles called 'Nine Maidens' or 'Nine Stones', which actually possess considerably more than nine stones. Actions associated with sites, such as running round a stone, usually have to be done three or nine times.

Other sites than stones, such as barrows, holy wells and churches, are also the subject of folklore.

❧

BELOW *Mitchell's Fold Stone Circle, Shropshire, which is the subject of many folk tales.*

Night Manoeuvres

~

One of the most striking and common folk stories is the 'church that moved by night' legend, which occurs throughout Britain. At Holme-on-Spalding-Moor in East Yorkshire, the church is sited at the top of a prominent hill and the village nestles at the bottom. The legend goes that the first church was started at the bottom of the hill, but during the night the walls were thrown down. This continued until it was realized that the fairies objected to the site, and the church was then built on top of the hill, which satisfied the fairies.[119]

SPIRITS OF PLACE

The Tale of Willy Howe
~

William of Newburgh, who lived in the twelfth century, records a folktale about the large Neolithic round barrow known as Willy Howe [on the Yorkshire wold]. A countryman was returning home late at night, rather drunk. From the mound, he heard voices of people singing, as if at a banquet. He went to investigate and, seeing an open door in the side of the mound, looked inside and saw men and women preparing for a cermonial meal. One of the attendants offered him a cup: he did not drink from this but threw out the contents and ran off with it. He was pursued, but escaped. The goblet was of unknown material, unusual colour and of unfamiliar shape: it was presented to the King.[100]

BELOW *In China, the dragon represents the spirit of the Earth.*

Ancient sites have traditionally been recognized as the haunts of beings or entities from worlds other than the everyday. Ghosts, fairies, dragons, giants, the devil and visitors from space have all been brought in at one time or another. These stories occur world wide.

There are several different theories about fairies. In one guise, they are the descendants of an earlier race inhabiting these islands ('the little people'), who retain their pagan faith and haunts, such as remote barrows and stones.

Ancient peoples and those living in country districts must have been more sensitive to nature spirits, or the entities underlying physical form. These can manifest, through interaction with the observer, in a form acceptable to that observer, hence local variants, such as 'boggarts' in Yorkshire, or 'traditional' fairies with wings. I shall look into the processes involved in a later chapter.

According to tradition, many sites, both natural and artificial, were formed by giants or the devil. A typical legend is that attached to the Hole of Horcum, a great natural hollow, and Blakey Topping, a prominent cone-shaped hill, both in the Yorkshire Moors. The devil, or alternatively the giant, Wade, is supposed to have scooped out the hole during a quarrel with a neighbour, and thrown it at his adversary. As the earth and stones landed they formed Blakey Topping.

Major earthworks are often said to have been formed by the devil, and standing stones to have been thrown by him, a famous example being the Devil's Arrows near Boroughbridge in Yorkshire.

The anthropologist Margaret Murray used to say that the god of one religion becomes the devil of the next[98], and these legends may be a way of indicating that the sites to which they were attached had been sacred in pre-Christian times. Many places known to have links with the old religion have 'devil' names, such as the rock outcrop called the Devil's Pulpit at Tealby, Lincolnshire.

There are legends of dragons throughout Britain. A typical one is the dragon of Nunnington, in Yorkshire. The hero, a knight named Peter Loschy, went to do battle with the dragon. He managed to sever segments of the dragon's body which his dog took away in its mouth. The head was poisonous, however, and the dog died as a result, but not before having licked his master, who consequently also fell dead.[115]

This story has many of the motifs common to dragon legends. Dragons were powerful, with poisonous breath. They often fought each other and attacked humans until slain by a brave hero, frequently at an ancient site. They often coiled themselves round hills.

That China also had dragons is interesting. The Chinese approach to landscape, including the forces underlying their concept of dragons, will be examined in the next chapter, which may enable parallels to be drawn with British examples.

PULLING THE THREADS TOGETHER

I started by postulating that there was a grain of truth in all folklore and legend. Having looked at some of the main elements of folklore as they relate to sites in the landscape, the question must now be asked: what does it all mean?

Let us take a quick look again at what has emerged. Any disturbance to the stones may have a direct and dramatic effect on the weather. On occasions stones appear to glow, and strange sounds emerge. Loss of balance, dizziness and tingling can result from close contact with the stones, but this can also have a positive effect on the health and fertility of people brought into such contact. These phenomena are associated with key points in the yearly, monthly and daily cycle, such as midsummer, full moon and midnight. The stone circles appear to have had some sort of tradition of dancing, perhaps associated with these key times.

The view that has found favour amongst those involved with Earth Mysteries, and one which seems to spring out of the page when these legends are brought together, is that most folklore associated with ancient sites can best be interpreted in terms of the survival of the old pagan religion and, one of its wellsprings, the existence of some form of energy which the ancient people were sensitive to and which they used for healing and in their rituals.

It is fair to say that this view is controversial: certainly Grinsell remains strictly factual, but the Bords support this explanation and in so doing follow in the footsteps of John Michell, Tony Wedd and earlier writers of the 1930s. It may not be a correct interpretation, but a better one has not been put forward. Undoubtedly, it does form an integrated web of ideas and, whether right or not, provides a framework within which folklore and legends can be assessed.

So, looking again at these legends with a possible energy explanation in mind, we can postulate that, in the case of healing, it is the energy which heals, particularly with repeated movement in one direction and prolonged contact. The legend of the White Cow of Mitchell's Fold (see page 28) indicates that the energy is not inexhaustible and could be permanently depleted if used unwisely.

Legends about the movement of stones arise because, if the stones are alive with energy, this in some ways affects our perception so that we feel they are moving. The same applies to tales of the stones turning round, rocking, dancing, and promoting dizziness. Legends about stones glowing, tingling and emanating sound also fit into an energy theory.

Similarly, the energy at sites may interact with certain individuals to create altered states of consciousness, which enables them to see more easily the variety of legendary entities which traditionally inhabit such locations.

The importance of certain times of the day, month or year suggests that the energy fluctuates according to cosmic cycles, and the rituals followed this. It seems from folklore that these involved dancing with music through the night, often on the Sabbath, and the legends about being turned to stone imply disapproval of the old pagan religion which kept up these practices.

In all these accounts, what emerges is that, at some time in the past, people were aware of energy at ancient sites. This awareness goes back a long time, and to trace it we need to go back into the realms of ancient philosophy.

BELOW *Legends of dancers being turned into the Merry Maidens Stone Circle, Cornwall, may well have their origin in memories of the old pagan religion.*

4

EARTH
ENERGIES

The evidence from folklore that some form of energy is associated with ancient sites in general and stones in particular was the starting point for a research effort initiated in 1977 by Paul Devereux, editor of *The Ley Hunter*. This was known as The Dragon Project, which he describes as 'a non-intrusive multi-disciplinary and multi-mode way of trying to understand the enigmatic stone monuments of prehistory'. Part of the programme involved monitoring known physical energies at the Rollright stone circle in Oxfordshire, including ultrasound, radiation, magnetism and radio emissions. Resources were limited, and any conclusions must be tentative, but there was evidence of cyclical variations in the energies being monitored and on a significant number of occasions the values detected inside and outside the circle differed dramatically.

EARTH LIGHTS

A parallel project, personally undertaken by Devereux, has been the investigation of what he has called 'earth lights'. These are light phenomena produced from the body of the Earth, particularly in areas of faulted geology, on mountain peaks and ridges, bodies of water and areas of mineral deposits. They are difficult to explain within the laws of electromagnetism. He considers that many occurrences of phenomena to which we give diverse names like UFOs, ghosts, will-o-the-wisps, and apparitions of various sorts, may all be manifestations of earth lights.[23,25]

Some areas have persistent earth light phenomena, such as Marfa, in south-west Texas. The first written account dates from 1883. White, yellowish and orange lights the size of a baseball have been reported moving around, sometimes performing aerobatics. They have been seen to spring suddenly into existence, to change shape, merge and split.

In the 1970s, together with Andrew York, Devereux made a study of his native Leicestershire to see whether there were any correlations between various phenomena, geological features and ancient sites. They found a high degree of positive relationship between areas of faulting and abnormal meteorological events, including reported UFO sightings and activity.[36]

An expanded study, covering the whole of Britain, showed a close correlation between UFO sightings and areas of tectonic activity. In addition, every stone circle in England and Wales was found to be within a mile (1.5 km) of a surface fault or on an associated intrusion.[23]

The energy which creates earth lights seems to have a sensitizing effect on people so that they are more likely to see things psychically, and there may be outbreaks of psychic effects, such as poltergeist activity. This latter has occurred in the vicinity of Hessdalen in Norway, where several hundred photographs have now been taken of earth lights, and where there is a permanent monitoring post.

The reverse also seems to be true: the energy plasma appears to be sensitive to psychic and thought forms, so that it can actually move or change shape according to the mind of the observer.

RIGHT *Marfa, in Texas, has been a focus for unexplained flickering lights for over 100 years.*

Marfa Mystery Lights
Over 100 years of unexplained flickering lights
Location: Mitchell Flats   Photo Date: 9/86
Photo Specifications: SLR w. 50mm lens at f1.8
Exposure: Less than 3 minutes Film: EL 400
Researcher/Photographer: ©1986 James Crocker

TEXAS
Marfa

A SUBTLE ENERGY?

The basic question is whether the reports, research results, anecdotal evidence and folklore refer to some form of known energy which can be easily integrated into the fund of established knowledge, or whether they indicate some other, more mysterious, perhaps more fundamental, energy, which operates in an altogether different way. Devereux is open on this question, though he admits that we know of only some of the 'invisible and subtler forces that course through creation' and even those we are beginning to discover can occur in contexts with which we are unfamiliar.

The existence of a fundamental 'life energy' has been postulated for thousands of years in many different civilizations, and crops up independently from sources which had little contact with each other.[138]

Its characteristics are remarkably consistent considering the wide cultural span, and are suggestive of some reality behind the accounts found in ancient philosophy, esoteric writings and the work of researchers into the unorthodox. Such writings hang together in a remarkable way, and one is left with a definite feeling that they are describing a real energy with specific and consistent characteristics.

One of the earliest descriptions is of the 'life energy' known as *prana* given in the ancient Hindu and yoga teachings. *Prana* is seen as a universal energy which flows in currents in and around the body. Other energies, such as heat, are seen as manifestations of *prana*, rather than energies in their own right. *Prana* can be inhaled and directed by means of currents flowing down the sheaths of the nerves to all parts of the body. It is present throughout the universe, the flow of energy into and out of the body occurring particularly at the energy centres known as *chakras*, at the base of the spine, the sex organs, solar plexus, heart, throat, brow and the crown of the head.

Ancient cosmology refers to the ether, a fifth element filling all space, and conceived as a purer form of fire or air. The Druids called this Wouivre or Nwyvre, and in the northern tradition it was known as ond.

Hippocrates (c.460–377 or 359 BCE) was aware of this energy, which he called *Vis Medicatrix Naturae* (The Healing Power of Nature), and it was also known to the medieval alchemists as *munia* – the Vital Fluid.

The shamanic *kahunas* from Hawaii taught that there was an energy called *mana* which could flow over threads of shadowy body substance and could carry thought forms.

The physician Paracelsus (1490–1541) saw it as a 'magnetic' influence enabling people who possessed it to heal others, 'as perfume emanates from a lily'. His disciple Van Helmont described it as radiating within and around a person like a luminous sphere.

Anton Mesmer (1734–1815) enjoyed great popularity in treating people with what he called 'animal magnetism'. His pupil, D'Eslon, formulated laws under which animal magnetism seemed to operate: it was a

BELOW *The life energy of the body, flowing through and between the chakras has been known under many names.*

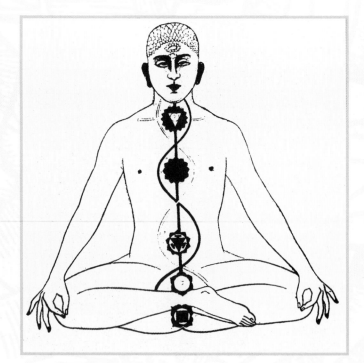

ABOVE *Wilhelm Reich studied the properties and effects of the life energy which he called orgone.*

BELOW *Kirlian photography records electro-biological energies, which may be the visual equivalent of Reich's orgone.*

universal, continuous fluid, which was subtle in that it had an ebb and flow; it was concentrated in the human body like a magnet; and could be accumulated and communicated over a distance.

In 1860, Baron Karl von Reichenbach (1788–1869) published the results of numerous experiments with sensitives using techniques which enabled them to sense an energy which he called 'the odic force', 'od', or 'odyle'. He began to realize that it was distinct from heat, electricity or magnetism, and gradually became able to describe its properties, which were very similar to those of 'animal magnetism'.[110]

In more recent times, the most highly developed exposition has been that of Wilhelm Reich (1897–1957). Although starting in psycho-analysis as a pupil of Freud, his work soon spread into what he saw as the related spheres of biology, physics, meteorology, astronomy and politics.

In his therapeutic work, he found that mental and emotional problems were often reflected in a patient's physical appearance, and began to think that emotions were 'locked into' the body by muscular tensions, a good example being the 'stiff upper lip' and the way that anger can be suppressed by a clenched jaw. Reich developed techniques for releasing these locked-up emotions by a combination of relaxation, breathing and massage. Working in this way, he realized that there was some unrecognized form of energy flowing through the body which was interrupted by muscular tensions. Reich developed therapeutic techniques which enabled the blockages to be dissolved and the body's energy to flow freely.

Did this energy have some objective reality or was it merely a way of looking at known processes from a different viewpoint? In 1939, Reich found evidence of it by 'chance' when experimenting with the creation of living cells called 'bions'. He found that they caused radiation effects such as reddening of the skin, conjunctivitis and the fogging of photographic plates, though tests showed that the level of traditional radiation was normal.

Further experiments with what he began to call 'orgone energy' demonstrated that it was present everywhere, in the atmosphere and particularly in living things. It seemed to flow from a weaker to a stronger system, thus acting contrary to the Second Law of Thermodynamics. It was always in motion, in waves and pulses, moving from west to east in the atmosphere. It could be observed in darkness as a flickering bluish-grey light; and there was a force in orgone energy capable of setting a motor in motion.[10]

Observing that orgone energy is attracted and absorbed by organic material whereas metal initially absorbs the energy and then repels it rapidly, he constructed a box with alternate layers of metal and organic material, starting with metal on the inside. This resulted in a build-up of orgone energy inside the box, dependent on the number of layers involved. He also found that sitting a person inside for a period each day helped the processes of healing.

More practical than a rigid accumulator is an orgone blanket, which can be made by sewing together layers of wool blanket and steel wool, covered by thin cotton. It can be wrapped around various parts of the body, with the steel wool side inwards.

THE SALMON LEAP

That this energy under its various names appears to have been recognized in diverse cultures yet be almost totally ignored by orthodox science is in itself very interesting. It draws us towards other ignored aspects of existence usually called the psychic, esoteric or occult and suggests a possible connection.

The essence of any claims for psychic phenomena or powers is that there are alternative realities to the physical. Earth Mysteries researcher, Brian Larkman, has reminded us that contemporary physics envisages 'virtual particles' which come into existence for infinitely small periods of time before disappearing. He postulates that such particles spend most of their time in a non-material or etheric state, momentarily leaping into the physical plane like a salmon leaping fleetingly into view above the water surface. He concludes: 'Such a process might be responsible for many of the phenomena of Earth Mysteries, indeed for most paranormal events which, like the salmon, are often extremely elusive.'[80]

BELOW *The salmon of knowledge leaping through the river of existence was a potent symbol in the Celtic tradition.*

There is a vast array of both scientific and anecdotal evidence for the existence of states of being other than the physical, and there are various ways of understanding such states. One is the 'Psychic Spectrum', whereby different levels of reality or 'vibrations' can be seen as equivalent to the optical spectrum of visible light. Some have put forward elaborate systems of 'planes of existence' varying from the densest physical to the highest (or deepest) realms. What is clear is that they are really describing a continuum rather than separate planes.

It seems as if all the universe, including the Earth and ourselves, is present at all points in this continuum, and that we are therefore truly beings at all levels.

It is reasonable to assume that ancient people were sensitive to the reality of these other levels of existence, living their lives accordingly, and it may be that we should look to this awareness as the origin of much of what we now label folklore.

Support for these other levels of reality has come from biologist, Rupert Sheldrake, whose 'Hypothesis of Formative Causation' has caused great controversy in scientific circles of recent years. As a result of investigating unsolved problems in biology, including how a seed or egg can contain the essence which grows into the new individual member of the same species, he postulated the existence of what must, by implication, be a non-physical mould or pattern, what he calls a 'morphogenetic field', which survives the death of the physical form, and which shapes the individual tree, animal and flower of each species, just as the individual field around a magnet can create a pattern in a scatter of iron filings. He suggested that these fields are moulded by the form and behaviour of past organisms of the same species through direct connections across both space and time, a process he calls 'morphic resonance'[116] This is something which has long been familiar to those with a spiritual or esoteric background.

THE SUBTLE BODY

Over thousands of years it has been recognized that the human body has a non-physical component, and it is striking that through all the descriptions there is a strong energy theme.

These subtler bodies, variously named etheric, astral and so on, can be seen by sensitives as an aura around the physical body. Dr Walter Kilner developed some screens filled with a dicyanin solution which sensitized the eyes and made it easier for more people to see the aura. These are available today in the form of goggles.[73]

The aura is an energy body. Within it, energy is transformed to and from the physical body through the medium of the *chakras.* These are related to vitality and sensitives can frequently see dis-ease here before it manifests itself physically.

Just as the blood is circulated through our physical body, so energy flows through and between the subtle bodies. Virtually all systems of healing recognize this energy flow, that dis-ease results from blockages, and that health can be restored by enabling the energies to flow freely. The technique of raising the *kundalini* is, in essence, allowing energies to well up the spine through all the *chakras* without obstruction.

ABOVE *Techniques have been developed which make it possible to photograph the human aura.*

LEFT *Water nymphs, or naiads, were considered to be the personification of water energy.*

RIGHT *The earth spirit can sometimes be experienced in human form.*

THE EARTH SPIRIT

There are many parallels between the individual human being and the Earth, and in the mid-1930s ideas began to be put forward about 'earth energies', linking the long tradition of life energy with the suggestion of place-related energies revealed in folklore. They also began to suggest strongly that leys were not just the traders' tracks that Watkins proposed but were closely associated with such earth energy, if not actually marking the channels along which such energy might flow. One of the first to do this was the occult writer Dion Fortune. In her book *The Goat-Foot God*, she mentions 'power centres': Tintagel in the west, St Albans in the east, Lindisfarne in the north, and St Albans Head in the south. She refers to the lines joining them as 'lines of force', and states that pagans worship the Old Gods on these rather than at the power centres themselves which had tended to have been 'exorcized' by the Christians by the erection of chapels dedicated to St Michael. She also says: '...where people

have been in the habit of reaching out towards the Unseen they wear a kind of track, and it's much easier to go out that way.'[47]

Another early writer on earth energies was Straight Track Club member Arthur Lawton. In 1938 he postulated that leys and pre-historic sites marked a network of subtle energy and that this power could be detected. He found the occurrence of certain standard distances and speculated that this was due to a 'cosmic force' creating a crystalline pattern on the Earth's surface.[81]

John Michell, writing of what he calls 'The Earth Spirit', states:

Rocks, trees, mountains, wells and springs were recognized as receptacles for spirit, displaying in season their various properties, fertilizing, therapeutic and oracular...Characteristic of the earth spirit, and in accordance with its feminine nature, is its tendency to withdraw, to decline within the Earth's dark recesses.[93]

LEFT *Tintagel Castle, Cornwall, reputed to be one of Arthur's seats, is one of the 'power centres' mentioned by the occult writer, Dion Fortune*

This ties in with archaeologist and dowser Tom Lethbridge's theory about the Earth's force-field being concentrated at certain natural features such as waterfalls, springs and streams. He thought that the human aura could interact with this force-field at such places. An individual in a certain state of mind could fix a powerful emotion to a place. Similarly, sensitives could pick up such an emotion at places that were so charged. He saw this as a possible origin of the nymphs of the elements which were known in ancient times – the naiads in waterfalls, springs and streams, dryads in trees and woods, oreads in mountains and deserts, and nereids in the sea.[57] Perhaps over the generations the interaction between a particular cultural context and the energy pattern at a place could build up a strong image or archetype.

One of the strongest corroborations of the existence of earth energies and the earth spirit has been the emergence of the concept of the Earth as a living being, given the name of the Greek goddess Gaia by James Lovelock, an independent scientist and thinker with a wide background of disciplines and experience. He is a prolific inventor who helped to start the environmental revolution. As a result of work undertaken for NASA, Lovelock studied the conditions necessary for the continued existence of life and found that the Earth constituted a self-regulatory system whereby each of the many variable factors, such as temperature and the composition of air, sea and soil, had been kept within the narrow limits necessary for life to survive for the entire history of the planet. It had all the required characteristics of a living being and Lovelock concluded that this indeed was what it was.[85]

This recognition has had a major impact, not only in the ecological field but also in that of Earth Mysteries. If the Earth is indeed a living being, it was argued, then it may possess a subtle body corresponding to the human aura, with *chakras* and flows of energy as well.

RIGHT *The Fairy Glen, Bettws-y-Coed , Wales, one of the spots where the earth spirit is strongly felt*

THE BREATH OF NATURE

What the ancient people experienced must largely remain in the realms of speculation, but we can look to China for a system which is still in use and very specific on the question of how earth energies relate to the landscape. It is known as *feng shui*, which means 'wind-water', and it will be examined in Chapter 8.[43]

Underlying the practice of *feng shui* is a recognition of the function of the energy which the Chinese call *chi'i*, or 'the breath of nature', in the health and well-being of a person; it is the fundamental princple underlying the ancient practice of acupuncture. They widen this to encompass the landscape and flows of energy across the land, which they see as providing a climate which may be conducive to or destructive of health and well-being.

They evolved a view of landscape which incorporated an awareness of the energy balance of a place, seeing *chi'i* flowing through the landscape, concentrating in certain spots, becoming stagnant in some places or dispersing from others.

The breath of nature can be seen as the interplay between the forces of *yin* and *yang*, flowing in currents known as *Lung Mei* (dragon's veins) around the countryside in winding paths, often following contours. These are seen in terms of two different, but complementary, energy flows, known as the Azure Dragon and the White Tiger, both aspects of the same energy, which need to be balanced. If the energy is blocked it can turn into what the Chinese call *sha*, noxious or torpid *chi'i*.

The form of the land determines whether energies collect or disperse. An accumulation of energy encourages growth, dispersal of energy results in barrenness. Too much

energy allowed to go stagnant and torpid results in death and decay. The *yin* landscape is a gently undulating plain, the *yang* that of steep slopes, mountains and outcrops. A desirable state is that of the two energies in balance, and the best site is located where there is a change from landscape expressing one type of energy to landscape expressing the other.

Where a landscape is dominated by *yang* forms, perhaps high in the mountains, the most desirable spot would be one that had *yin* characteristics. The site of Castlerigg stone circle in the Lake District is an example, where the plateau on which it is sited is surrounded on all sides by mountain peaks. Many stone circles are, in fact, to be found in such locations. Where there is a predominantly *yin* landscape, the favourable site would be one which had *yang* characteristics, such as Glastonbury Tor, or the sacred aboriginal site of Uluru (Ayers Rock) in Australia, both prominent features rising out of a flat plain.

Mountains where the 'dragon's veins' run close to the surface are powerful sources of *ch'i*. Mountain peaks are classified according

ABOVE *Uluru (Ayers Rock), Australia — a yang site in a yin landscape.*

to their shape, in terms of the five elements of fire, wood, water, metal and earth. Wood, for example, was represented by a flattened-off peak and fire by a pointed hill.

Ch'i flows along watercourses, the ideal being slow, sinuous and deep, as it is conducive to the accumulation of *ch'i*. Straight waterways and sharp bends draw *ch'i* away too rapidly. Confluences are good because there is a concentration of *ch'i* at that point.

Sloping, well-drained land is conducive to the right amount of *ch'i*. Badly drained and low-lying areas are best avoided. Trees help to keep a high level of *ch'i* and are usually favourable.

LEFT *A Chinese landscape showing characteristic yin/yang landforms.*

ELUSIVE FIELDS

Accumulated evidence from recent research, combined with ancient traditions, all help to build up the conviction that we are dealing with a real, but elusive, energy which people have recognized throughout history, and particularly at special places in the countryside.

There can be no definite conclusion at present about whether we are dealing with 'known' energies or whether the evidence suggests some more fundamental force underlying the various observed properties and manifestations. We are still woefully ignorant about the operation in the landscape of the whole range of natural energies that are known to exist. It seems likely that *ch'i,* for example, would cover a wide range of energy effects, and Paul Devereux has suggested that *sha,* the noxious form of *ch'i,* could actually be radon gas.[28]

Nevertheless, when all factors have been assessed, there still remain effects which cannot be explained in orthodox terms. The energy behind earth lights undoubtedly has electromagnetic properties, but there are other aspects of the energy, such as its ability to respond to the consciousness of the percipients, which suggests something else is involved.

Devereux considers that, at root, there is a substratum which can only be described as consciousness, that this is a field effect and that the brain simply processes the consciousness in a similar way to that in which a television set processes a transmitted signal.

He thinks that the ancient sites were locations where altered states of consciousness could more readily occur. Undoubtedly they were places with magnetic stones and high natural radiation – things much rarer than in our modern technological society. Indeed, according to Devereux, such is the state of our cultural orthodoxy that the consciousness field of the Earth, if that is what, at root, this subtle energy is, can really only be experienced in altered states.[28]

If we take Sheldrake's ideas about morphogenetic fields seriously (see page 36), we may have the suggestion of a hidden energy field actually underlying the formation of the landscape itself, giving it both form and character.

Must this remain speculation, or are there ways we can find out more about this mysterious earth energy? It is clearly something which requires more than just new methods of investigation – it needs a whole new approach.

5

FEELING
THE
EARTH PULSE

If earth energies exist, what can we find out about them? And how? Our methods should be appropriate to what we are looking for, and we should be clear what our motive is. My emphasis is not to prove anything. 'Proof' is a relative term, anyway, each individual requiring a different amount to be convinced. This may depend on their level of awareness, or, as Edward de Bono puts it in his Second Law of Thinking, what appears to be 'proof' is often no more than a lack of imagination in providing an alternative explanation.[22]

The scientific step-by-step approach is not the only way to proceed: to flow with creative and fruitful ideas is just as valid, and it doesn't matter that some ideas fail to meet orthodox criteria. A willingness to take risks and make mistakes in the process is, however, necessary. As we are part of our own subject matter, we ultimately find ourselves. Astrologers might link these different approaches with planetary aspects in the birth chart. Reichian analysis would see it in terms of our level of character armouring. If we prove something to our own satisfaction, we can release our energies for finding out about the subject: proving it to others takes second place.

I am in sympathy with the approach Tony Wedd advocated, which was to accept temporarily everything that was put forward, to work with it and see where it got you: the attitude of the technologist as opposed to the scientist. So I am going to suggest ways of finding out about earth energies and of understanding the processes involved, how the ancient peoples related to them, and how we may ourselves be able to build a stronger link.

The importance of a holistic approach, using both analytical and intuitive methods, is vital, and it is noteworthy that many of the leading figures in the Earth Mysteries field have been trained in both arts and sciences and see the fruitfulness of combining the two approaches.

ORTHODOX ARCHAEOLOGY

OPPOSITE Nine Stones, Belstone, Dartmoor, Devon.

BELOW Newgrange, Ireland. Archaeologists long ignored the local tradition about the significance of the midwinter sunrise

If we want to find out about ancient people and the sites they used and constructed, our first thought might be to consult the archaeologists. Much knowledge has been accumulated since the antiquarians first started to take an interest in ancient people and their sites. Archaeology has become an increasingly scientific discipline, using modern techniques such as aerial photography, which has vastly increased the number of known sites, and carbon dating, which has caused radical rethinking of accepted chronology and the subsequent revision of many established theories.

While a profusion of information has been revealed, archaeology has, by its very nature, been largely concerned with what is found physically, which tends to emphasize the mundane, domestic level of existence. It has been more difficult for it to investigate the non-physical nature of prehistoric society. The purpose of the vast megalithic constructions, for example, remains almost as mysterious now as it did in the nineteenth century.

Archaeologists are beginning to realize this and are looking at alternative approaches, seeing sites as part of the landscape and related to one another, something which has been advocated by students of leys and Earth Mysteries for many years. Prehistoric archaeology has immensely broadened its approach over the last twenty years.

Just as the archaeological establishment is slowly changing and a willingness to try new approaches becomes evident, so Earth Mysteries enthusiasts have begun to undertake archaeological training. But some of the most fruitful findings at ancient sites have been made by those such as the researchers on the Dragon Project discussed later in this chapter, trained in disciplines other than archaeology.

Despite these cautions, recent archaeological findings have provided much of value to the study of Earth Mysteries, particularly concerning the extent to which linear features were a prominent part of the prehistoric landscape, and the acceptance that monuments such as chambered 'tombs' had more of a ritual function.

INTUITIVE APPROACHES

We now know that the 'detached scientific observer' is a myth: we are intimately tied up with whatever we are observing. The distinction between the individual and what is being looked for can be confused: the problem is that we don't always know how much. It can be fairly clear when looking for something physical, but in trying to find earth energies there are difficulties in determining what comes from the individual and what from the site.

The psychic sense involves finding things out in other ways than by the normal physical senses. It is probably a lot more common than is generally realized, a background 'noise' which only becomes noticeable when emphasized to such a degree that we can no longer ignore it. An analogy might be the lip-reading that we do at an unconscious level. It is only when I take off my glasses that I realize the extent to which the skill is providing 'back-up' information.

Psychometry

Psychometry is the ability to discern something about an object or its owner by holding it and 'visualizing' its history. It is the purest form of finding out about an ancient site, but it does depend on the ability of the observer to distinguish between various streams of information that may be coming in from a variety of sources.

The technique is to allow through the first impressions that come to you. Don't filter them out because they seem silly, and don't be afraid of being wrong. If you are honest, approaching with an open mind and saying the first thing that comes into your head, you will gradually find you are able to contribute real information and will gain confidence in your abilities.

Psychometry can, of course, be extended from an object to a whole site. Here the technique is to wander round, touching the stones or whatever, allowing expression to whatever comes to you.

Any opening of oneself psychically, particularly at ancient sites which have a long and largely unknown history, can be hazardous, and it is best undertaken with caution and proper attunement. The whole question of approaching sites is covered in Chapter 11.

Psychic Archaeology

The most straightforward use of psychic ability is in finding archaeological remains which, at least, is something which can later be verified.

The method came to prominence through the activities of Frederick Bligh Bond, a highly respected authority on medieval church architecture. In 1908, he was appointed to excavate the remains of Glastonbury Abbey; and made use of the services of a friend, Captain John Bartlett, who, with automatic writing, brought through messages from monks who had lived at Glastonbury, together with detailed plans of the Abbey, showing a large, hitherto unknown, chapel at the eastern end, named after King Edgar.

RIGHT *Glastonbury Abbey, where Bligh Bond found the remains of a chapel by following psychic messages*

Two years later, Bligh Bond started excavations and found the Edgar Chapel, in the position and of the size predicted. When the story was published, he was dismissed from his post, and had great difficulty raising money for further excavations.[9]

Archaeology, in the sense of deciding where to excavate, is perhaps a good example of where the psychic ability may often be used unconsciously. Even dowsing is obliquely referred to in the official reports as 'probing with metal rods'!

Psychic Quest Work

This has had much prominence in the Earth Mysteries field, but is somewhat difficult to define. In its archetypal form it involves tuning in psychically to past lives, to artifacts hidden in the countryside and to issues not resolved in the past. The method has all the elements of a fictional adventure story, and yet it cannot be dismissed so easily. It seems as if there were people in medieval and earlier times, aware of the significance of particular sites, who have, in some way we do not fully understand, left instructions and clues which can be followed by those who can tune in to them.

Dowsing

Go on any Earth Mysteries trip to an ancient site and it is highly likely that you will see at least one person walking holding wire rods or holding a weight on the end of a piece of string. You might even see more elaborate devices. What on Earth is going on?

All these people are doing is using their psychic faculties. They are, however, making use of a tool to help them just as a botanist might use a magnifying glass. The instrument acts like an amplifier to enable subtle mental or physical responses to be noticed. However elaborate the equipment, it is merely magnifying the natural psychic ability (or lack of it) that the individual might have. It implies nothing else: dowsing is not inherently more reliable than any other method involving the psychic senses. The presence of equipment does not change that. Dowsing is not more objective than more obviously and directly 'psychic' methods, particularly where it is concerned with detection of earth energies rather than physical artifacts, water, and so on. Pennick and Devereux are blunt on this point: 'The dowsing rod has become an implement to authorise the acceptance of subjective ideas as factual statements.'[105]

ABOVE *Fingal's Cave, Staffa, Scotland. This is said to mark the end of the Giant's Causeway that once linked Ireland and Scotland. It inspired the composer Felix Mendelssohn to write his overture 'The Hebrides'.*

LEFT *Dowsing at Sancreed holy well, Cornwall.*

Dowsing Techniques
~

Dowsing has a long history. The traditional hazel rod was a freshly cut forked stick, held in both hands by each 'fork', in some tension, so that a slight movement of the hand could result in a large movement of the rod. These days, most dowsers use angle rods, which can be cut from a wire coat-hanger, each rod bent at right-angles. It is useful to bind the ends with drafting tape to avoid accidents! Hold them loosely in each hand with the long arms straight ahead. Adjust the angle with your wrists so that a small movement will cause the rods to cross.

That is the mechanism: what you have to do is use it. Focus the mind as precisely as possible on what you want to find and start to walk. When you find what you are looking for that part of you which knows more than the conscious mind will send a message to the muscles in your hand, which will cause the rods to cross. That is all there is to it: the skill is in being clear about what you want to find.

The pendulum consists of a weight on the end of a piece of string, thread or chain usually a few inches long. It is more often used indoors. You hold the end of the string and the muscles in the hand cause the 'bob' to gyrate or swing in pendulum fashion. The pendulum can thus be used to answer yes/no type questions. One interesting application is map dowsing, where the map, as a representation of the landscape, can be dowsed in substitution for the real landscape. The technique is the same: move a pointer over the map with one hand and dowse with the other.

Dowsing and other devices, including the various 'ley detectors' invented by Jimmy Goddard,[53] appear to be a way of bringing this general psychic awareness into focus, demonstrating it in a form which our conscious mind can handle. Dowsing depends on the interaction between the person and the site at a particular time. The fact that different dowsers can get very different results on the same site can perhaps be explained as the interaction between their own energy field and the field of the site, so that the dowsing patterns found can only have true meaning by looking at the dowser as well. The dowsing response can tell as much about the dowser as about the site under investigation.

The knack in dowsing is to be in the right frame of mind, not caring too much what answer you get, but at the same time having a clear idea of what you are looking for, otherwise you are opening yourself up to a very wide 'waveband' and things will get very confused.

This is the difficulty in dowsing for earth energies. We are all familiar with water, as our bodies are mostly made up of it, and it is the easiest thing to dowse for. Even with minerals and lost objects we have a reasonably clear idea of what we are looking for and the dowser can be proved right or wrong. When it comes to earth energies, we really have no idea.

Most dowsers have attempted to find the patterns of earth energies at a site and have detected spirals, concentric circles and straight or sinuous lines, all of which seem to vary over time.

Perhaps the best way to use dowsing in Earth Mysteries is to look for something definite – a lost markstone, for example, or an alignment. Immediately we get into dowsing for 'energy', whether it be lines or points or spirals, we have a problem of tuning in to what we want to find. The 'waveband' is just too wide. I am not saying that natural energy flows do not exist, but to detect them alongside the multitude of artificial energy sources, and the thought forms of everyone who has visited or passed through the site, is likely to be confusing, to say the least. At any rate, treat all results with the greatest of caution, and don't make too much of them.

Dowsing has been used in association with more traditional ley-hunting techniques. An example is the Pitch Hill ley project organized by the Surrey Earth Mysteries Group. A line was initially dowsed: when plotted on a map, it was found to fall on an alignment of sites which was then followed and dowsed. Even here, the possibility of detecting a wide range of different effects is high.

There is no generally agreed explanation for how dowsing works and some consider that the answer lies in emanations from whatever is being sought. One thing is clear, however: it does work! I have seen Water Board engineers using angle rods to locate a water main, presumably because it was more effective than relying on plans, which are apt to be inaccurate, and easier than trial and error.

But to conclude the subject of dowsing and intuitive ways of finding out about ancient sites, the only way is to have a go yourself.

Your first visits should just be a matter of getting to know the site, by wandering around. Let the site itself tell you what is there, and then follow your natural impressions. Try dowsing without rods: it's much less cumbersome. Imagine them: it works just as well.

THE DRAGON PROJECT

Despite its limitations and difficulties, dowsing was one of the sources of inspiration for the Dragon Project, which I mentioned briefly at the beginning of the last chapter.

In 1975, the author Francis Hitching was commissioned to write a book and television documentary entitled *Earth Magic*.[69] He had made contact with various people involved in the field and arranged to meet veteran dowser Bill Lewis, who took him to the 12ft (4m) high Llangynidr standing stone near Crickhowell. Lewis had dowsed a spiral of energy on the stone which he found varied over time.

He asked Hitching to find out whether this could be detected scientifically. Hitching contacted John Taylor, Professor of Mathematics at King's College, London, who suspected that Lewis might be responding to small changes in magnetism. To measure the strength of the magnetic field, he supplied a gaussmeter which was to be operated by the young Argentinian physicist, Dr Eduardo Balanovski. He found a very strong field on and around the stone, much greater than background levels. On testing the bands of energy which Lewis had marked on the stone, Balanovski found the field to be twice as strong as on other parts of the stone.

Monitoring of this sort seemed to offer a way forward. When Paul Devereux took over *The Ley Hunter* in 1976, it was widely assumed that some form of energy existed at ancient sites, but there had been virtually no research to back these ideas up. In November 1977, a meeting of interested individuals from different disciplines was called to discuss the possibility of establishing some sort of research programme. The group included

physicists, materials scientists, dowsers, psychometrists, electrical engineers, psychologists, artists and other Earth Mysteries workers. (Incidentally, it is interesting to note that this occurred only five days after the discovery of the planetoid Chiron, the astrological meaning of which includes the collaboration of previously separate and antagonistic disciplines.) The philosophy right from the start was to incorporate a variety of approaches, both analytical and intuitive. The work fell naturally into two sections: physical monitoring of known energies led by Dr Don Robins, a materials scientist and specialist in piezo-electricity in archaeological research; and the psychic approach, including dowsing and psychometry, co-ordinated by Californian archaeologist and parapsychologist, John Steele. The programme would be known as the 'Dragon Project', after the Chinese representation of earth energies. Its objectives, published in 1978, were 'to

BELOW *The Rollright Stones, scene of the Dragon Project experiments.*

detect, by quantifiable physical and biological means, the manifestation of 'earth energy' at prehistoric sites and to relate this to the ultimate nature of earth energy and to the suspected prehistoric manipulation of this energy'.[26]

Because of limited resources, efforts were initially to be concentrated on a particular site. This would have to be convenient for London, where most of the participants lived, and, in view of the unorthodox nature of the enterprise, preferably in private ownership. The Rollright stone circle in the Cotswolds fitted the bill perfectly. It was a 100ft (30m) diameter circle, with stones, made of limestone, up to 7ft (2m) tall. In addition to the circle, there was the King Stone standing stone and the Whispering Knights, a dolmen in close proximity. Grinsell describes it as having 'one of the richest collections of folklore of any British prehistoric site'. Crucially, it was within 100 miles (160km) of London and the owner, Pauline Flick, was willing to allow the programme to proceed, and to occupy the hut on the site.

The physical monitoring started with very little clear idea of how to proceed. Lines of enquiry suggested themselves from reported material which had accumulated over the years on possible energy effects at ancient sites. An example was ultrasound, suggested by a zoologist whose colleague's 'bat detector', which receives sound in ultrasonic frequencies, had picked up a strong signal emanating from a nearby ancient site.

The approach of the Dragon Project to energies was straightforward. We may be dealing with an energy currently unknown to science, but it made sense to start by monitoring known energies. They may provide a clue by their behaviour even if this turned out later to be merely the secondary effect of some more fundamental energy.

The range of physical monitoring undertaken by the project has been extensive, and I can only briefly indicate below the main features of this and the conclusions so far reached.

Ultrasound

The instrument used initially was a wide band receiver in the 25–80kHz range, adapted from a 'bat detector'.

In autumn 1978, ultrasonic pulsing at two-second intervals was recorded at dawn at the King Stone. In December that year, there was one occasion when within the circle there was not even the normal background level which could be detected outside. This 'zero-field effect' has not been repeated.

There was an outburst of ultrasonic pulsing in February 1979, starting 8–10 minutes before sunrise at new moon and 25–35 minutes before sunrise at full moon. The effect would continue through sunrise and up to 2–3 hours afterwards. This gradually lessened through the spring and disappeared completely in the summer. There was no equivalent pulsing recorded at the 'control' sites being monitored.

In January 1987, a clicking signal at 37kHz was detected coming from a band 3ft (93cm) wide halfway up the tallest stone in the circle. The effect diminished half an hour after sunrise, but was repeated at noon.

The pattern of ultrasonics at Rollright has so far remained elusive.

ABOVE *The Rollright Stones produce variable ultrasonic pulsations.*

Radiation

Radioactivity exists naturally, emanating from the rocks, particularly granite, that make up the Earth's crust and also in cosmic rays from space. There are various ways of monitoring radiation, the best known being the Geiger counter. Initially, the project had use of a very basic one which involved the manual counting of audible bleeps, which could then be averaged to counts per minute.

Many other sites as well as Rollright have been monitored and the general conclusion so far is that there are radiation anomalies but they vary over time and that only an intensive continuous study at a site is likely to reveal the pattern. Some sites have radiation levels higher than the general background in the area, but there is a tendency for Cornish circles to be below background. Some, such as the Merry Maidens, have specific parts which are above background level and others which are below. Robins found that Geiger readings there were halved when taken within a few feet of the ring of stones, as if the ring acted as a form of 'shield'.[111]

In 1983, the Gaia Programme was set up in conjunction with the Association for the Scientific Study of Anomalous Phenomena (ASSAP). Scores of volunteers took part in ten-hour sessions, monitoring radiation at and in the vicinity of 30 sites and control locations. Results show a much greater variation of readings at stone circle sites compared with the control locations, but, for the patterns and cycles involved to be defined, long-term continuous monitoring at numerous sites will have to take place.

BELOW *The Whispering Knights Burial Chamber, near the Rollright Stones, was the site of several monitoring exercises under the Dragon Project.*

ABOVE *The Merry Maidens generate fluctuating levels of measurable radiation.*

Magnetism

Balanovski's earlier findings at the Llangynidr Stone in Wales suggested that magnetism might be a line of enquiry worth pursuing, though efforts were frustrated for some time due to the failure to obtain the necessary equipment.

An interim experiment took place in 1981 with tubes of brine shrimp, which are sensitive to changes in the magnetic field: they seemed to cluster at the end of the tube which was nearest the stones.

Then, in 1982, independently of the Dragon Project, Charles Brooker, a retired BBC engineer, carried out a magnetic survey of the Rollright Stones. He found that the intensity of the magnetic field within the circle was lower than that outside. He also found a spiral of relative magnetic intensity: two stones on the west side of the circle were pulsing magnetically, in cycles varying from 40 to 60 seconds.[13]

Later, the project was able to borrow a more advanced flux-gate magnetometer and the preliminary conclusions from Rodney Hale, an experienced electronics engineer, as a result of further work, are that there is a magnetic field within the circle which fluctuates relative to that outside over a period of hours.

Photography

An infra-red photograph of the King Stone taken in April 1979 at sunrise showed a glow around the stone and a 'ray' sloping off from it which photographic experts have not been able to explain.

A photograph taken by Devereux in January 1986 of a larger stone on the western side of the circle, which had been the subject of short-term magnetic anomalies, showed a discharge from the top of the stone.

Radio reception

Generally, a broad-band radio receiver works best with the receiver held in the air, with the signal fading away when the aerial is brought

❧ RIGHT *Energy effects have been experienced at many sacred sites, including The Devil's Den at Preshute in Wiltshire.*

near the ground. However, at highly localized areas around (but not within) the Rollright circle, another signal could be picked up almost at ground level. Analysis of the signal demonstrated its artificial nature but its behaviour remains unexplained.

Assessment

While much work remains to be done, energy anomalies do seem to exist at prehistoric sites. As Brian Larkman remarks:

❀

This is vital information for any understanding of prehistoric motivation and vastly increases the range of data available from a ceremonial site. It is time for many such ideas to be amalgamated into a fresh overview of prehistory; time for them to be applied holistically. Conventional archaeology must now be seen as only one aspect of a balanced study of prehistory, not the dominant factor.[79]

❀

In more recent years, the work of the Dragon Project has extended from Rollright to dozens of other sites throughout the country, including 'control' sites. Paul Devereux has chronicled the results of these studies in his book *Places of Power*[26] which showed that the recording of anomalous phenomena was by no means limited to Rollright. Resources, however, have been severely limited and the emphasis latterly has been to identify types of site where further studies might prove most fruitful.

To this end, in 1987, the Dragon Project Trust was set up to continue the work of the project, details of which can be found on page 47. With the limited resources available, efforts have been concentrated on finding what Devereux has called 'the Mind-gates of Gaia' – those special locations where the geophysical environment can most easily enable individuals to experience altered states of consciousness. These include rocks with a high proportion of quartz, zones where natural radioactivity is strong or places which have specific magnetic peculiarities. The effects on consciousness at sites with specific geophysical anomalies are looked at in more detail in Chapter 9.

One specific example of ongoing research in this area is 'Operation Interface'. This originated from the realization that one traditional worldwide practice is that of sleeping at particular sacred sites in order to benefit from the prophetic or divinatory content of dreams or from contact with spirit entities. Celtic seers wrapped themselves in animal hides near a waterfall or spring to achieve this and in the Graeco-Roman world it was known as 'dream incubation' or 'the temple sleep'.

There are many techniques for achieving altered states of consciousness, such as rhythmical drumming, dancing, fasting, ingesting hallucinogenic plants, etc. One factor that has so far not received the attention it deserves is that of the site where the consciousness-altering ritual or ceremony takes place. This seemed to be something which could have a profound effect on consciousness.

The purpose of the study was to look at this aspect. Four sites which have acknowledged geophysical effects, including Carn Euny *fogou* in Cornwall and Carn Ingli mountain-top in Wales, were chosen and volunteers were asked to go there in pairs at night. One

would sleep (in a specially warm sleeping-bag) and the other (the 'therapeute', to use the traditional term) would watch and, when signs of rapid eye movements (an indication of dreaming) occurred, would wake the sleeper to enable their dreams to be tape-recorded. These would then be put on a computer database and eventually analysed by Dr Stanley Krippner, Professor of Psychology at Saybrook Institute, San Francisco, a world authority on dreaming and altered states of consciousness.

The objective of all this is to see whether any site-specific dream imagery occurs. While the project is still ongoing and therefore no details have been released, Devereux has indicated that they do seem to be getting some quite startling recurring images emerging in dreams experienced by different people in at least one of the sites.[29,31]

This concentrated effort at trying to establish evidence for the interaction between people and site seems to be a fruitful way forward and, coupled with the insights revealed in Chapter 9, is likely to prove to be one of the main directions forward for Earth Mysteries during the next few years.

BELOW *The entrance to a* fogou *at Carn Euny Iron Age village, Sancreed, Cornwall.*

6

RESPONDING
TO THE
EARTH

The term Earth Mysteries covers not just ancient sites but also the people who visited them and found them significant in their lives. We too are part of the whole subject area ourselves: our own relationship to the sites and the Earth is vital. Responses to the Earth can be immensely varied, and looking at the various ways people have responded to the natural energies manifesting at ancient sites is central to any theory that attemps to explain or enlighten the mystery.

Paul Devereux sees the whole field of Earth Mysteries in the form of a tree. The top of the tree consists of ways in which we can sense, such as archaeology, psychometry, dowsing and aesthetic response. The next layer of the tree integrates major areas like geomancy, which will be discussed in the next chapter. The point at the top of the trunk is occupied by the single theme – 'energies'. The trunk represents the site itself and the roots are the living Earth beneath the site.[28]

In many ways, the area at the top of the tree parallels a structure called the 'Spectrum of Response' which I described in 1985.[80] The degree of interaction between observer and energies is reflected in the spectrum and I have divided it into six strands: experience, attunement, ritual, interaction, manipulation and control. Clearly these merge into each other, but they range from, at one extreme, the individual who visits an ancient site, becomes aware of the energies and then goes on their way to, at the other extreme, those who try to control the earth energies and use them for their own ends.

The further along the spectrum we find ourselves, the more we need knowledge and wisdom to be able to handle the results. It is really a question of how much we see ourselves as part of or in conflict with nature. Modern society tends towards the latter end of the spectrum, feeling that it has to 'control' nature in all its many aspects.

As well as providing a useful way of looking at people's response to the Earth through the physical structures which have survived, and as a way of interpreting legend, the Spectrum of Response is also a framework into which we can fit our own relationship to the landscape.

DIRECT EXPERIENCE

OPPOSITE *Gypsy Encampment near Furness Abbey by Samuel Bough (1822–1878). Gypsies and people who regularly walk the country's paths are often more sensitive to the fluctuation of Earth energy than more sedentary urbanites.*

BELOW *Cave with aboriginal designs at Uluru (Ayers Rock), Australia.*

Like any faculty, the psychic sense is more prominent if it is used and if the society in which an individual lives is conducive in its attitudes to the encouragement of such ability. The traditional peoples in the world today, such as the Australian aborigines, are profoundly and naturally psychic and it is at least reasonable, therefore, to speculate that the ancient peoples were similarly sensitive, and would have been aware of earth energies as a natural part of their environment. Brian

Larkman has shown that, properly translated, orthodox anthropological writings can be read in such a way. He gives the example of the Walbiri tribe of western central Australia. They recognize two states of being: *Yidjaru*, which relates to the material world, and *Djugurba* which equates with the non-material. They see the landscape as being formed by 'dreamings', which came into the material world at so-called 'waterholes', which may or may not correspond to an actual waterhole. The dreamings follow a set path as they alter the topography, leaving their potency, or *Guruwari*, at specific points en route, before disappearing back to the non-material world at the point where they came in. He writes:

> *It seems to me that they are describing at first hand a world made up of physical materials similar to those which we can see and touch, with an invisible (to most of us) non-material life force much like the ether superimposed on it and within it.*[77]

The way in which earth energies are experienced seems to vary according to cultural expectations, so that pure energy is interpreted in ways acceptable to the individual or culture. This seems to be the case with reported visions of the Virgin Mary, identification of whom usually occurs after the initial vision, which is frequently witnessed by children, outdoors, at springs or streams. In France, at La Salette, children saw a bright light near a stream, then a lady who appeared and disappeared. At Lourdes, Bernadette Soubirous saw what she described as 'that thing', which was thought to be the ghost of a local girl.[24]

Paul Devereux, in the context of earth lights, suggests that the percipient may have a real effect on how the energy actually manifests. The intensity and character of earth energies also seem to fluctuate according to the time of day, month and year. When combined with the sensitivity and psychic state of the experiencer a whole range of possibilities opens up.

Direct perception by psychics of energy manifestations in the landscape has a very long history. It merges into folklore, myth and legend. In modern times, many people have claimed to be able to see fairies. The theosophist Geoffrey Hodson gives detailed descriptions of various elemental beings which he had the ability to observe in various natural locations.[70] While the famous photographs of the Cottingley fairies, taken in 1917, have been admitted not to be genuine, it is equally clear from the researches of author Joe Cooper that at least one of the girls concerned, Frances Griffiths, did see fairies in Cottingley Glen, as did Geoffrey Hodson.[18] Ogilvie Crombie, known as 'ROC', also acquired this ability, perhaps by living alone in a forest for ten years, and was able to contact nature spirits, including a being identified as the Great God Pan.[45] He was closely associated with the community at Findhorn, in Scotland, where Dorothy Maclean and, subsequently, several others, were able to make contact with the *devas* – higher level beings embodying the essence of a particular species or, in particular cases, of a place.[87] Detailed guidance was frequently the result of such contact. This seems very similar to Sheldrake's concept of the morphogenetic field and to Lethbridge's ideas on the formation of the nymphs of the elements.

ABOVE LEFT *Visions frequently occur near water, where psychic sensitivity seems greater.*

LEFT *The photographs of the Cottingley fairies, now admitted to be fakes, were inspired by genuine sightings of fairies at the nearby glen.*

ATTUNEMENT, INSPIRATION AND ART

Attunement as used here means more than the
mere experience (of earth energies) and
implies some response – often called artistic
inspiration and expression. But first, how do
we experience landscape? Appleton considers
the major factor to be the ability to see
without being seen.[2] It may also be our ability
to respond to energies in the landscape, such
as the Chinese describe in their concept of
ch'i (see Chapter 4). The attraction of a
landscape to an individual will thus be a result
of energies, however defined, running
through both the individual and the observed
landscape.[65,66]

In order for earth energies to inspire, the
individual needs to be in a place where, and at
a time when, those energies are strong, and
also needs to allow such energies to flow
freely through them. We can 'tune in' to these
energies more easily at particular places than
others, and it is actually easier to meditate, for
example, at such places. The climate is better
for the raising of perception or, in poetic
terms, the veil between this world and beyond
is thinner.

Landscape and the sacred sites within it can
be both an inspiration for art and the stage on
which that artistic expression is played out. In
this sense all ancient people were artists as
they lived their whole lives in harmony with
the Earth, but were they artists in the more
conventional sense?

Certainly some of their art, such as cave
paintings, survives and may provide a clue as
to how they thought. In Britain, rock art was
a major feature, consisting frequently of cup-
and-ring marks. These are usually made up of
a central pit or cup, surrounded by one ring
or concentric rings or spiral turns. There are
occasional more elaborate designs such as on
the Tree of Life Stone near Otley, Yorkshire.
The marks are usually found on rock outcrops
at the edge of upland moors, particularly in
the Galloway, Clyde and Argyll areas of
Scotland, Northumberland and Rombalds
Moor in Yorkshire. Although the greatest
concentration seems to be in Britain (perhaps

ABOVE AND BELOW *These rock carvings from County Donegal are typical of many to be found in Ireland, Scotland and Northern England.*

LEFT *Rock carvings at High Banks, Galloway.*

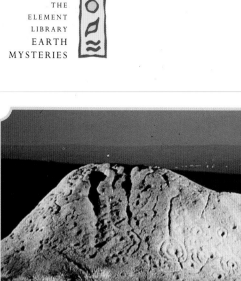

While the forms of inspiration vary, the individual needs to attune to the 'atmosphere' of the place, so that it can encourage the artistic and creative faculties to respond and generate output that is deeper, finer and more prolific than otherwise.

Many artists, poets and composers have drawn inspiration from the landscape and have felt the need to visit sites. Sometimes this is clearly reflected in the work of art produced, sometimes the connection is more indirect. The composer, Edward Elgar, for example, needed the solitary paths of the countryside around the Malvern Hills and often spoke of hearing songs and sounds not heard by others. He used to say: 'I think music is in the air all around me: I've only to take as much as I want'.

This immersion in the landscape is the technique used by poet and Earth Mysteries researcher, Ian Taylor, before writing his book, *The All Saints' Ley Hunt*.[120] He walked every ley until the landscape started to speak to him.

only because Britain has been searched most thoroughly), this type of design is found throughout the world.

Many different explanations have been put forward, but the similarity of many of the cup-and-ring carvings to such diverse phenomena as lines found by dowsers and the symbols used to describe sacred places in Australia and elsewhere, suggests strongly that they represent aspects of the non-physical reality which ancient people could see. Brian Larkman has speculated on their significance:

The very act of carving the symbols in the rock can create an electrical charge which could be seen by a sensitive. Such an idea catches the imagination: stones that glow and sparkle as the curving patterns are chipped and pecked into them; circles and cups and lines that not only symbolise some holy and sacred place, but that pulsate with the life of the earth dancing her spirit across their surface. It is just such a spirit that would be wanted to animate the fertility of the earth and ensure the continuance of increase and plenty in the plants and animals that a browsing existence depends upon. How better to release it than to ritually carve the sacred pattern each year, close to the slowly fading illuminations of earlier ceremonies.[80]

Paul Devereux[24] has drawn our attention to the Irish nature mystic, George William Russell (who wrote under the pseudonym AE). He was aware of the earth spirit, and seemed consciously able to tune in to what he called 'earth memories' and 'the memory of nature'. Under certain states of consciousness he could become aware of the subtler dimensions of the landscape and wrote:

※

These earth memories come to us in various ways. When we are passive, and the ethereal medium which is the keeper of such images, not broken up by thought, is like clear glass or calm water, then there is often a glowing of colour and form upon it, and there is what may be a reflection from some earth memory connected with the place we move in or it may be we have direct vision of that memory...[113]

※

There are artists whose inspiration and field of action is the landscape itself. One of the best known is Richard Long. His work typically consists of some form of activity in the countryside, which is then recorded by a photograph or map. He has, for example, created a visible straight line across grass by repeated walking; walked a ten mile (16 km) dead straight line across Exmoor; walked all the roads and tracks within a six mile (10 km) radius of the Cerne Abbas giant; walked from Stonehenge to Glastonbury on Midsummer's Day; and created cairns, stone circles and labyrinths at specific sites in the landscape.[50] He has never admitted an awareness of Earth Mysteries as an inspiration for his work, but the walking of straight lines echoes not only leys but also the task of the Gaia Programme monitors who were required to take regular readings on straight lines out from ancient sites.

The work of Andy Goldsworthy must also be mentioned. He uses natural materials in the natural landscape and, by arranging them, draws attention to their significance, such as forming decaying leaves into a pattern which emphasizes their variation in colour. His photographs of these works are freezing a changing process in time.

Photography has a central place in the Earth Mysteries field by virtue of Watkins' status as a Gold Medallist of the Royal Photographic Society. This feel for his native countryside comes through strongly in his photographs; person, camera and landscape being in creative harmony. He considered that the best-composed photographs were taken 'along the ley'. Photographs say something, often very subtly, about how the photographer sees and relates to the landscape. Through this relationship, they can also be a record of the life force that exists at a certain site.

Artists such as Jill Smith and Bruce Lacey have developed the idea of performance at sacred sites both as an artistic expression and also as a form of ritual whereby the artist may be inspired to receive insights into the original purposes behind sacred sites.[76]

Bob Trubshaw poses the question: 'Is the act of visiting an ancient site a piece of performance art?'[24] To use the landscape itself as the stage or background for artistic expression takes us to the very boundaries of art until, as we step across, we realize that the whole of life is, or could be, Art.

LEFT *The Badger Stone on Rombalds Moor, West Yorkshire, shows the characteristic hillside location typical of such rock carvings.*

※

BELOW *The Malvern Hills, which form the boundary between Herefordshire and Worcestershire, have provided inspiration for many, including the composer Edward Elgar and the antiquarian, Alfred Watkins.*

RITUAL

In essence, ritual is very simple. In the context of ancient sites, it involves becoming aware of the special nature of the place and taking some action, however small, in recognition of this. Guy Ragland Phillips gives an example:

Annabel, the daughter of a friend, paid us a quick visit from the other end of the country. We took her to see the Three Howes, prehistoric mounds on the summit of the moors. From the road she followed the track alone. After a while, sitting in the car, we saw her stand for a few minutes first on one of the Howes, then on another, still and with arms raised. She was in prayer.[108]

Ritual can therefore be an individual, spontaneous activity, but society and tradition are also important factors. Folklore suggests that dancing took place at stone circles on occasions such as the seasonal festivals. Much of the significance of ancient sites comes from their use for ritual purposes, and this is borne out by the survivals of ancient traditions. Certainly witches still have a tradition of performing rites at special places in the countryside and it seems natural for people to want to express their relationship with the Earth in the form of ritual at sites where they know the earth energy can be found.

The 'climate of the place' is, however, only one part of the equation: the other is the state of mind that the person brings to it. This is where ritual may come in, making it easier to attune to the energies. Witches, for example, have a series of rites aimed at achieving this result, including the casting of the 'magic circle' to keep the power from dissipating.

The use of ritual, which may involve dancing, psychoactive plants and other techniques, may be directed towards the achievement of altered states of consciousness or to specific ends such as healing. Alan Bleakley tells of some very fruitful rituals including working with archetypal images which have taken place at various stone circles in Cornwall.[8]

RITUAL ROUTES AND SACRED SITES

The form and position of stone circles, tree clumps and wells strongly suggest a ritual approach along an ancient trackway, as if walking the paths that others have trod before encourages the energies to manifest. This may correspond with a ley or may be something of a more sinuous nature. Michell elaborates on this:

The ways between these places…are ways of the earth spirit, not merely secular routes but natural channels of energy, first traced out by the creative gods, followed by the primeval wandering tribes and still in settled times used by religious processions or pilgrims to a shrine. Traditionally they are also paths of psychic activity, of apparitions, spirits of the dead or fairies, particularly on one day of the year. People of the Irish countryside recognize certain lines, unmarked on the ground, as fairy paths, lines of a seasonal flow of spirit, which must on no account be obstructed or built on.[93]

Certain paths also had a teaching function. The custom of 'beating the bounds' by taking children around the parish boundary and beating at significant points, in order that the children should remember them, is a reflection of this. Before people could generally read, learning was by word of mouth and much took place in the countryside along the paths, particular truths being imparted at certain places, which thereby took on special significance. Walking the paths was thus a ritual act, what the Buddhists might call 'walking meditation', and the paths themselves reflected this importance. A deeper understanding of the function of leys might emerge if they could be seen in ritual terms.[131]

ABOVE *The seven petalled rose and cross is the symbol of the Rosicrucians, a mysterious secret priesthood.*

BELOW *A traditional Buddhist tanka, the 'Wheel of Life', in the grasp of the demon Mara. The Buddhist tradition is rich in ritual and meditation.*

SECRET TRADITIONS

Invaders bring their own religions and practices and in Britain particularly the old traditions had to go underground. Ancient knowledge of the existence, significance and power of particular places was preserved in secret as it would not have been acceptable to the Church or society at large.

There are many strands to this secret tradition, and one of the most direct and striking is that of witchcraft. Most modern witch covens can be traced back only as far as the revival stimulated by Gerald Gardner and the repeal of the Witchcraft Acts in the 1950s, but there still exist traditional covens which date back much further. The beliefs and practices of witchcraft, with an emphasis on the cycles and hidden aspects of nature, the special significance of places, and the generation by such means as dancing of the 'cone of power' within a magic circle from the energy residing within the human body, tie in very well with the insights obtained through Earth Mysteries research.

Other traditions also kept ancient knowledge alive. Gypsies and other travelling people retain an instinctive awareness of the significance of sites and the flow of subtle energies through the seasons in a far stronger form than more settled people. It is tempting to imagine an exchange of information and assistance between gypsies and witches, both being subjected at times to severe persecution.

Within Christianity there have always been strands, such as the Templars, Cathars and Rosicrucians, that have retained an awareness of the old secrets. Writers such as Paul Screeton and Andrew Collins have speculated on the existence of an 'inner priesthood', whereby certain churches on particularly sacred sites have specially selected clergy. More recently the Freemasons and the various magical orders have continued certain traditions.

It is a testimony to the fundamental nature of pagan beliefs and practices that they have survived centuries of persecution. What has also survived, at least in part, is a landscape which has been moulded according to those beliefs.

Seasonal Customs and Rites

~

From ancient times, the significance of particular dates has survived centuries of attempts to stamp out the old pagan customs, and they are still popularly practised in many parts of the country.

The ''Obby 'Oss' tradition in Padstow, Cornwall, takes place on May Day. Many villagers take part, and the place is decorated with flowers and branches. The festivities start the previous night, the hypnotic beat of the drum and the traditional song having a very strong effect. The 'obby 'oss itself is a huge circular black 'skirt' with a sharp-beaked head which whirls around supported by a team of dancers.[58]

The village of West Witton in Yorkshire holds the ceremony of the 'Burning of Bartle' on the Saturday nearest to 24 August, St Bartholomew's Day, to whom the local church is dedicated. An effigy of Bartle, said to be a medieval sheep thief, though undoubtedly a much older figure, is paraded round the village after dark and then set alight.[121]

Many other pagan traditions still continue or are being revived. They are the public face of the secret survival of ancient belief and practice tied up with the power of the landscape.

Imagine a trackway, winding across a hillside, no more than a sheep track, perhaps, or an ancient drove road. Every person or animal that follows the path seems to leave a trail of energy, and these energy paths build up over time. At intervals along the path the energy intensifies. Here animals stop to rest or to give birth, and individuals pause for momentary contemplation. Each occurrence at such a spot builds up the energy store until, after generations, it begins to be noticed more consciously. A standing stone is erected or a tree planted, followed generations later by a wayside cross, church, inn or even village. Or perhaps the subtle energy with which the place is charged will encourage the growth of a tree or the thickening of a hedge. These are spots sanctified by time, and thus are some sacred sites born, the result of the interaction between people and the landscape: instinctive working with earth energies to increase the significance of place.

7

GEOMANCY
AND THE
CREATION OF FORM

The instinctive, artistic and ritualistic responses to the earth energies are not the only ones. There is also the path of geomancy, where actions are taken which can affect the quality of the physical environment and, as a consequence, the inner being.

The mystic and the magician are examples of contrasting approaches. The mystic seeks to experience the unity of existence through a variety of practices and environments: essentially, the approaches examined in the previous chapter were examples of the mystical path as revealed in the landscape. By

Stourhead at Stourton in Wiltshire is an example of a landscape that has been aritificially created by the building of mounds and the sinking of lakes.

contrast, the magician seeks to understand the energies of the universe and to work with them in order to bring about changes, ultimately within the self, but including the environment in all its aspects. This distinction between mystic and magician is helpful provided we realize that the two archetypes can be combined.

This chapter looks at geomancy and the variety of ways, of which the magical approach is but one, in which people have modified their environment in order to achieve inner change.

SACRED GEOMETRY

ABOVE *Trinity,*
the three-fold, is a
central concept in
Christianity. The idea
of the three-in-one is
often found expressed in
the details of church
architecture.

ABOVE *The power*
of triplicity was also
revered in pre-Christian
times and much Celtic
decorative art uses
the device of three
interlinked symbols.

ABOVE *A formal*
pattern of interlocking
fish, an important
symbol in both Christian
and Celtic traditions.

One major strand of geomancy is sacred geometry. As soon as people began to build artificial forms and structures, sacred geometry came into being as the pattern, conscious or unconscious, underlying a particular structure. The name is somewhat misleading, since in ancient times it seems likely that the division of life into 'sacred' and 'secular' had no meaning: the whole of life was considered sacred, as were artistic and other creations.

The creation of structure was for a purpose: the hermetic principle of 'as above, so below', imitating the macrocosm in the microcosm, bringing the vastness of nature and the universe down to a scale to which human beings can relate.

Form can create 'atmosphere' and one of the main functions of artificial structures is to create an environment in which change of consciousness can more readily occur.

The essential forms of artificial structures stem from an awareness of the way in which the principles of shape, proportion, number, measure and relationship occur in nature. Straight lines can be found in shadows, rays from the sun or moon or their reflection on water, the stem of a tall grass, rock strata or a clear waterfall. The circle can be seen in the discs of sun and moon and their related haloes and rainbows. More complex structures are revealed in crystals, and precise proportional relationships may be found in the arrangement of leaves and branches and the spirals of growing shoots.

Shape

The effect of shape on function is recognized in sacred geometry. All the fundamental shapes were used – the straight line, circle, triangle and square revealed in leys, stone circles and the elaborate structures in mediaeval churches – together with other shapes of more esoteric symbolic significance, such as the pentagram, the hexagram and the *vesica piscis*.

The six-pointed star, consisting of interlocking triangles, is a form often used in sacred geometry.

Proportion

Proportions of all kinds exist in Nature, such as the relationships between the daily, monthly and yearly cycles. Two of particular significance are the Golden Mean and the Fibonacci series. The Golden Mean is the division of a line such that the smaller part is in the same proportion to larger part that the larger part is to the whole. It is approximately 1:1.618 and has been recognized by artists throughout history as being uniquely harmonious. It is also represented by the relationship of the sides of a pentagon drawn between the points of a pentagram and the sides of the pentagram itself. The Fibonacci series is produced by adding together the last two numbers in a sequence to get the next number – 1, 1, 2, 3, 5, 8, 13, 21, 34 and so on. It is found underlying much natural form, from the shape of horns to the pads on a cat's foot.

The principle of proportion is at the heart of our aesthetic awareness and close to the life principle controlling plant growth. Artificial structures have used such proportions for both these reasons and probably also because of their effect on sound and subtle energies.

Number

The principles of number are at the heart of the universe. The nature and character of unity, twoness, threeness and so on underlie the whole of existence. Astrologers have probably come closest to understanding these principles in their use of planetary aspects and in the theory and techniques of harmonic astrology, pioneered by John Addey.[1]

We have already noted that folklore associates certain numbers, particularly three, seven and nine, with prehistoric sites. Other traditions, such as military regimes and cultures with a central control, are based on the division of land by means of the cardinal directions and subdivision by halving, resulting in a fourfold and eightfold division.

In astrology, the two-series of aspects (2,4,8 etc) is connected with the way we relate to the outside world, whereas the three-series (3,9 etc) is more about internal harmony; this may provide a clue to the meanings underlying the use of number in sacred geometry.

Measure

By analysing distances in stone circles, the surveyor Alexander Thom believed he had found a unit of measure, of some 2.72ft, which he called the 'Megalithic Yard', though this has since been demonstrated to be unlikely.[122] Traditional measures are based on average lengths of different parts of the body, and are related to each other in terms of significant numbers such as three and twelve.

ABOVE *The seven-pointed star is particularly related to inspiration and practical design.*

THE USE OF GEOMANCY

The ancient people were well aware of the way in which the principles of sacred geometry were a reflection of Nature. In creating artificial forms they were not only careful to ensure that their siting was appropriate but also that all the elements in the design, such as shape, proportion and size, respected Nature rather than acted against it. It is because these principles have been lost that much modern architecture is criticized: there is no link with or respect for Nature.

The skills required to use such awareness to create artificial form are those of the geomant – a combination of shaman, geographer, town and country planner, sculptor, architect, artist and landscape designer.

Geomancy, sacred geometry and magic all aim to achieve effects, both in the individual and the outside world, using the energies of the universe by flowing with them. This is similar to technology, which aims to make things happen rather than to find out why they happen.

But this is no ordinary technology: we are dealing with the subtle energies which flow through the Earth and which have their own ways and seasons. Tony Wedd invented the word 'allotechnology' for this form of technology, as it is different in kind and basic principles of operation from that which is presently dominant in our society.[136] He accumulated information on a variety of devices from different sources, including claimed contact with people from beyond this planet, and was able to elucidate certain basic principles, including the use of 'free energy', no moving parts and the importance of shape, number and materials to proper functioning. If one person was involved in making the whole device themselves, it would work better for them, because it had been impregnated with their own vibrations. This is similar to the old traditions associated with making magical tools.

The evidence seems to indicate that the ancient people operated some such technology to effect changes in earth energies.[56]

BELOW *An antiquarian engraving of the Carnac alignments in France shows them sadly toppled and neglected. Since then, they have been repositioned to follow as closely as possible the alignments devised by the original geomants who set them up.*

Magic Circles

The circle is one of the most fundamental shapes in nature. It is seen in the form of the sun and the full moon, halo and rainbow. It is also one of the easiest shapes to construct.

Witches and other natural and ceremonial magicians still use a magic circle. It may be marked out on the ground, but the true circle is that which the magician creates mentally. It is in reality a cross-section through a sphere. Its function is two-fold: to protect against outside influences and to contain the power that is raised by the magical practices carried out within.

There is no direct way of knowing whether the ancient people constructed magic circles, since by their nature they are only temporary. But we do know that the most obvious surviving monuments, the stone circles, take that form, and we can at least speculate that they may have performed a similar function. The effort involved in constructing such circles was enormous. They were obviously very important, and it follows that their function was too.

We have certain clues, such as the folkore tradition of dancing at key dates and times in the year, and the importance of the type of stone used, some, for example, being pure quartz. They were constructed carefully, sometimes as exact circles, sometimes as partial ellipses. There were probably astronomical alignments. The siting of the circles was often on a saddle with a good view round to neighbouring hilltops. Conclusions from the Dragon Project suggest that in some cases the stone circles can act as a 'shield' from outside energies. (See chapter 5 for more detail.)

From what we know of modern witchcraft practices, we can speculate that the stone circles were used for dancing and that this was a method of raising power (similar to the 'cone of power' that witches use today) which could then be stored in the stones to be used when required. This would explain the great effort expended in moving the stones long distances to their designated sites: they had a specific quality and function.

A tradition that still survives is that of the native people of North America. Their 'medicine wheels' have much in common with the stone circles of western Europe. At least 50 are known, stretching from Colorado up into Canada. They can be up to 200ft (60m) in diameter and are mostly constructed of stones, with a rim, and spokes radiating out from a central cairn. The Big Horn Medicine Wheel in Wyoming, for example, has a 12ft (4m) diameter central cairn and 28 lines of stones radiating as spokes. There are also five smaller cairns around the rim which have been found to indicate astronomical alignments. The 28 spokes suggest a link with the lunar cycle.

BELOW *Medicine Wheel at Sedona. Arizona, USA. These structures made by Native Americans seem to be linked to the cycles of the moon.*

ARCHAEO-ASTROLOGY

ABOVE *The link between stone circles and the rising and setting of sun and moon has long been recognized, as here at the megalithic alignments of Carnac, Brittany.*

With an unpolluted atmosphere and skies free from any city glow, together with a naturally heightened awareness of the totality of their environment, the sun, moon, stars and planets were an important background to ancient people. Sensitivity to the forces lying beneath the surface, seeing subtle connections between parts of the landscape that seem separate to us, would lead them inevitably to what we would call a form of astrology. Rather than call it 'primitive', I prefer to see it as direct, relating what happened on the Earth directly with events in the heavens. This astrology did not reside with ephemerides or in computer programs, but in personal daily knowledge of the movement of heavenly bodies through the sky.

In this, I think, is to be found the origins of and impetus behind the arrangement of sites, the study of which has gone under the name of astro-archaeology, or, more recently, archaeo-astronomy. Both are based on the same belief: that ancient people throughout the world set out their mounds, standing stones and stone circles in a particular relationship to each other and to the natural features of the landscape such as hilltops and notches, so that lines were set up to mark significant dates of astronomical events in the annual and other cycles. Referring back to what I see as the purpose behind the whole

practice, I have called it 'archaeo-astrology'.

Perhaps the best-known example is that of the Heel Stone at Stonehenge. From the centre of the circle, it was long believed to mark the midsummer sunrise, to which the avenue is also aligned. The antiquarian, Stukeley, noted it in 1740, and it is quite possible that knowledge of this never died out locally. In Ireland it was also generally known that the rays of the sun at winter solstice sunrise illuminated the chamber of the ancient mound at Newgrange. The relationship of this with the other mounds in the Boyne Valley area has been the subject of detailed investigation by Martin Brennan, who has demonstrated purposeful and exact siting and orientation.[12]

In the early 1960s, American Professor of Astronomy, Gerald Hawkins, analysed the positions of the stones at Stonehenge by computer and calculated the extreme rising and setting positions of sun and moon in 1500BC. He found 24 significant alignments. He further suggested that the 56 Aubrey holes could have been used as eclipse predictors, representing three cycles of the moon's nodes, each taking 18.6 years.[62]

Alexander Thom, formerly Professor of Engineering at Oxford, had been visiting stone circles since the 1930s making very accurate surveys. He found that only two-thirds are true circles: the rest are flattened circles, ellipses and egg-shapes, all made, he believed, with relatively simple geometric construction, though this has not been subsequently confirmed.[122]

He also found that many of the stone circles were associated with other features some distance away, such as a standing stone, hillside notch or rock outcrop, and that the lines to these features had astronomical significance. The most crucial test of this was at a standing stone at Kintraw, Argyll. Thom said that midsummer sunset was observed from a small platform on a steep hillside overlooking the stone. Euan MacKie excavated the platform and found that it was artificial.[86]

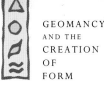
MAZES AND LABYRINTHS

Another pattern to be found in our landscape is that of the maze or labyrinth. Most people are familiar with the hedge maze, the most familiar example in England being the Hampton Court Maze, dating from the late seventeenth century. This type is multicursal – in other words, there is a choice of routes. It is possible to get lost: indeed, that is the whole point of the thing! There is, however, an earlier type of maze, which is laid out as a pattern on the ground, either with stones, cut into turf, or as a pavement. It is unicursal: there is only one route – a single convoluted path leads eventually to the centre.

Labyrinths of this type have been found inscribed on tombs in Egypt dating to 3400BCE, and the same design occurs on the Cretan coins of the Minoan period, though it may have originated in much earlier times. Carvings to this pattern, thought by some to date from 1500BCE, have been found in Rocky Valley, near Tintagel in Cornwall.

There is a tradition, central on the Scandinavian countries, of labyrinths formed with stones and small boulders, the only remaining example in Britain being on St Agnes in the Isles of Scilly.

In Britain, the tradition of turf-mazes is predominant. There are two distinct types: the older pagan type and the more elaborate Christian version which consists of four sectors in the format of a cross. Over a hundred are known to have existed, and there may have been over a thousand at various times. They were well known in Shakespeare's time, for in *A Midsummer Night's Dream*, Titania remarks about a period of unseasonable weather:

❧

The nine men's morris is fill'd up with mud,
And the quaint mazes in the wanton green
For lack of tread are indistinguishable.

❧

Being cut in turf, they need to be maintained or they would disappear completely within a generation. Many were destroyed by the Puritans and only eight now remain.

Making Mazes
~

It is not difficult to construct your own labyrinth, either in stones or cut into your lawn. Essentially the method is to make it in stages in accordance with the diagrams. Stones can be moved around until you get it right, but on a lawn the pattern should be laid out with pegs initially.

ABOVE *Lay out a line on the ground subdivided into 15 and draw out a basic grid as shown.*

LEFT *Draw arcs through the subdivisions of the original line, centred on two corners of the grid.*

RIGHT *Then round off the corners to finish. When you have the pattern as you want it you can dig out the edges.*

Surviving Mazes
~

The Walls of Troy turf maze near Brandsby, North Yorkshire, is possibly the most ancient in Britain, though it has been re-cut on several occasions, most recently in 1934, when carts using the grass verge had obliterated it. It is still being tended regularly.

Julian's Bower, at Alkborough, Lincolnshire, is altogether more elaborate, having twelve concentric circles. It is based on the pattern in Chartres Cathedral (below) dating from 1118. Up until 1800 the tradition survived of treading the maze on May Eve.

ABOVE *Julian's Bower, Alkborough,
Lincolnshire, one of the few surviving turf mazes.*

Maypoles
~

*A maypole dance in the sixteenth century
by Joseph Nash 1854.*

Another pagan survival is the maypole. Many villages, such as Barwick-in-Elmet in Yorkshire, retain the tradition of erecting the pole and dancing round on May Eve and at other times. Tom Graves has speculated that the wooden pole may have been the equivalent of the standing stone – a 'needle of wood' – and that its action was encouraged, or primed, by the performance of fertility rites.

What was the purpose behind mazes and labyrinths? The similarity of their design to cup-and-ring patterns is striking and suggests that they may have had a ritual function. This appears from the evidence of written records, folklore and surviving illustrations to have involved dancing and walking – as an act of penance or, more fundamentally, as a means of attuning or meditation. As generations followed the pattern of the maze, the earth energies may have illumined their forms in just the way that they may have done with the cup-and-ring marks and the pilgrim's tracks.

It is natural to walk or run them and anyone who has done this will know that it becomes more of a rhythmic dance when perfectly attuned. Certainly there was, within recorded memory, a tradition of dancing, and witches are known to have used them as meeting-places. The act of turning, of moving towards and then away from the centre, has the effect of disorientation and loss of balance, as in some 'trust games' and initiatory rites, and can bring the fluctuating emotions of despair, hope and surprise. The labyrinth is yet another way in which consciousness can be altered.

SUBTERRANEA: THE WOMB OF THE GODDESS

We have seen that the stone circles may have performed some function of protection and concentration – creating a special 'atmosphere' within which ritual or other activities could take place.

A further development from this idea is that of the totally enclosed chamber. Natural caves are the most obvious; some of the earliest evidence for permanent dwellings comes from caves, and they also seem to have had some ritual function, connected with ancient cave paintings. Bob Dickinson draws our attention to the sensitive placing of such paintings in relation to points of resonance in the caves of Ariège in the French Pyrenees.[39] The ancient people seemed well aware of the qualities of the spaces and acted accordingly.

People have also constructed artificial underground chambers since the most ancient times, the native American *kivas* and the Cornish *fogous* being examples. There is also a suggestion that in Britain the elaborate chambered tombs and long barrows, and such structures as Newgrange in Ireland, were not just used for burial but for other purposes as well. The cromlech at Pentre Ifan in Wales was known in folklore as 'the womb of the goddess Ceridwen' and was used for initiations.[71] There is evidence that, in the *kivas* at least, psychoactive plants may have been ingested.

These purposes are linked to the functions of the magic circle we have already seen – of protection and concentration – but with the true three-dimensional nature of the 'magic sphere' revealed. John Michell was the first to draw attention in print to the similarity

ABOVE *The womb-like underground room of a surviving Iron Age* fogou *in Cornwall.*

❧

BELOW *This* kiva, *or underground ritual room, in Colorado, USA, helps create an atmosphere conducive to shamanic practice.*

between such structures, with their layers of organic (earth) and inorganic (rock) material, to Reich's orgone energy accumulators (see p. 35).

Light phenomena have been observed in and around these locations. Devereux mentions the experience of John Barnatt and Brian Larkman at Chûn Quoit in Cornwall where they saw an unexplained flickering of coloured lights on the underside of the capstone.[26]

The mind is naturally drawn here to such activities as the 'temple sleep' and shamanic initiation practices, and to modern sensory deprivation chambers. If someone were to be left alone in one of these structures, not only would the physical senses be deprived, but the individual would be in a psychic atmosphere well suited to the encouragement of inspirational and prophetic experiences.

Church crypts may well have had their origin in such chambers. This is clearly seen in the crypt at Lastingham in North Yorkshire, and I have personal experience of the power of this place. The crypt is very simple, built right into the hillside. Some years ago, I visited the church with a friend. She felt such powerful energies in the crypt that she was unable to speak. She said afterwards that she had never experienced anything like it, but that it was not unpleasant or fearful. I also experienced the sensation, but in less pronounced form. It was as if the energies

within my brain and body were reacting to the energies within the crypt and a flowing, pulsing feeling of warmth came over me, somewhat similar to my feeling after a session of Reichian therapy. I was unwilling to move for many minutes as I experienced the power present in that place. After perhaps ten to fifteen minutes the feeling faded, although I also did not wish to speak and I made my way outside.

Later, I took the then editor of *The Ley Hunter*, Paul Screeton, there. He got a buzzing feeling and thought the place quite extraordinary. Afterwards, he was to write: 'If you want to get a feeling of what ley power is like, go into the crypt at Lastingham church, and it'll change your life.'[114]

When Ian Thomson and the current editor of *The Ley Hunter*, Paul Devereux were doing fieldwork for their book *The Ley Hunter's Companion*, they visited the crypt and found that the needle of their compass maintained a strange rhythmic 'jigging' motion.

BELOW *Many have experienced powerful energies in the ancient crypt beneath Lastingham Church in North Yorkshire.*

ABOVE *The Celtic church seemed aware of the presence of the earth spirit at the sites which they chose to build.*

CHURCHES

RIGHT *The Druids in
their sacred oak grove.*

Whether the first church buildings were
Christian or pagan is probably a matter of
semantics. Certainly we know from Pope
Gregory's instructions that temples existed
and were reused by the Christians. It is also
certain that while the leaders of a community
may have, possibly for political expediency,
formally converted to Christianity, most
people retained their pagan beliefs and
practices.

Guy Ragland Phillips has shown the extent
to which pagan symbols, such as the Green
Man, *shiela-na-gig*, pentagram and the like,
survive in ostensibly Christian buildings.[108]
Ian Taylor draws attention to the church
building as a continuation of the Druid groves:

*Christian churches were modelled upon them, the
pillars and arches representing the trunks and
boughs of the sacred forest. Pre-Reformation
churches were painted in imitation of the colours of
the woodland, from which gods and elementals
looked out upon the worshippers.*[120]

BELOW *This
figure, known as the
Sorcerer, comes from a
cave painting at Ariege,
in France. It may
well represent a
fertility dance.*

It seems certain that hidden teachings on
sacred geometry – form, shape, proportion,
number, measure and materials – were passed
on into Christian times and were incorporated
into much church architecture,
including the great cathedrals.
Church architecture of the
medieval period demonstrates
a high level of awareness of
the effect of form on
consciousness. All the principles of sacred
geometry were applied in their
construction. The circle was used,
and round churches, though
rare, are a distinct form.

The more elaborate
geometry of the hexagram
(two equilateral triangles,
superimposed on each
other), the pentagram
(the symbol of the
witches), and the *vesica
piscis*, was also used.

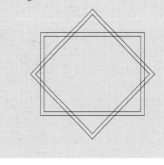

Triangles and Squares
~

Most churches were laid out on the basis of
equilateral triangles and squares, the so-called
'*ad triangulum*' and '*ad quadratum*' methods. *Ad
quadratum* is basically one square laid over
another at an angle of 45°, and has been one of
the commonest systems employed throughout
the world. *Ad triangulum* is based on the
equilateral triangle, the finest example in
England being King's College Chapel in
Cambridge.[102]

8

POETIC GEOGRAPHY

Most subjects have an established body of knowledge to fall back on, but Earth Mysteries, though rapidly evolving, is still in its infancy and is alive with ideas and speculations on forms and energies in the landscape. These have been, in many cases, the living threads out of which the subject area has been woven, but many must now be recognised as being subjective flights of the imagination.

Earth Mysteries is maturing and it is now possible to have a somewhat clearer view of how these ideas and speculations fit into the total picture. As stimulations to the imagination, they may help us to gain deeper insights into the true nature of our relationship with the living Earth, but we need to be clear as to whether we are dealing with objective landscape artifacts or something internal to the percipient which has been projected out onto the landscape.

In this chapter I deal with several speculative ideas and concepts, many of which have not stood the test of time as independent realities. They may help individuals to understand and relate to the landscape, but that must clearly be seen as a separate thing.

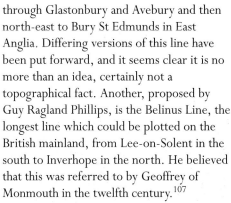
LANDSCAPE GEOMETRY

Josef Heinsch saw sacred geometry and what he called sacred geography as being part of a continuum stretching out from the structure and form of the building into the surrounding countryside. Many have postulated a geometrical pattern across the land, using sacred measure and proportion, extending Watkins' ley theory into wider concepts of 'landscape geometry', and we have already looked at the work of Tyler, Lawton and Koop in exploring wider patterns.

Leys over 60 miles (96 km) long began to be claimed[129] and soon lines of several hundred miles, such as Dion Fortune's 'St Alban's Cross', began to be described, while Kenneth Koop publicised the claim that Arbor Low stone circle in Derbyshire had over 100 leys passing through it.[75]

In 1970, I put forward the concept of 'primary leys': a structure into which all other leys were supposed to fit. One example is the 'St Michael Line' first put forward by John Michell, which was purported to run from St Michael's Mount in Cornwall,

through Glastonbury and Avebury and then north-east to Bury St Edmunds in East Anglia. Differing versions of this line have been put forward, and it seems clear it is no more than an idea, certainly not a topographical fact. Another, proposed by Guy Ragland Phillips, is the Belinus Line, the longest line which could be plotted on the British mainland, from Lee-on-Solent in the south to Inverhope in the north. He believed that this was referred to by Geoffrey of Monmouth in the twelfth century.[107]

One large scale landscape pattern which John Michell has drawn attention to is the Circle of Perpetual Choirs, mentioned in the Welsh Triads as being located at Stonehenge, Glastonbury and Llantwit Major. These three places are equidistant and, if taken to fall on the circumference of a circle, can be seen to form three points of a decagon, the centre of which falls on the hamlet of Whiteleafed Oak, where Worcestershire, Herefordshire and Gloucestershire meet.[91]

The trouble with all these lines is that, aside from the problems associated with the curvature of the Earth, there is virtually no evidence for them as leys of any description. Indeed, the very idea of a major structure or grid into which leys have to fit says more about our own cultural environment than the reality of the landscape.

Some have gone much further and postulated grids covering the whole of the Earth's surface. Steve Cozzi defines a planetary grid system as 'any series of lines laid out across the surface of the Earth in an attempt to measure some particular pre-designated system of ideas, correlations or theories'.[20]

There is within us all an urge to make order out of seeming chaos. The wish to discern a framework for the Earth itself is something which dates back at least to the time of Ptolemy. Most of the many suggested grids bear little relation to each other and even less to the landscape, showing more about the human addiction to order than allowing the Earth to show her own organic nature.

❧

OPPOSITE AND BELOW St Michael's Mount, Cornwall and Bury St Edmunds Abbey, Suffolk (below), two points on the purported 'St Michael Line'.

TERRESTRIAL ZODIACS

Katherine Maltwood was a sculptor with an interest in folklore and mythology. In 1925, on reading *The High History of the Holy Grail*, she realized that the places mentioned corresponded to sites in the Vale of Avalon, Somerset. She plotted them on a map.

In a moment of inspiration, she found something else: 'I shall never forget my utter amazement when the truth dawned on me that the outline of a lion was drawn by the curves of the Cary river, below the old capital town of Somerset'.[89] A giant, outlined by Dundon and Lollover Hills, followed. An astrologer suggested that these represented Leo and Gemini. From that moment on, Maltwood gave herself to the search, eventually finding the signs of the zodiac, arranged in a circle ten miles (16km) across, with effigies outlined by rivers, streams, roads, tracks and contours, with earthworks at key points. She believed that the figures had been laid out in prehistoric times as a form of temple or sanctuary, using the natural forms of the landscape with a minimum of artificial alteration.

Maltwood wrote several books about what she called 'Glastonbury's Temple of the Stars', and over 60 other zodiacs have now been claimed to exist, with a great variation in the figures as well as in size, shape and orientation.[64]

But is there any real evidence that such zodiacs are anything more than the product of an overactive imagination? There is certainly deep within all of us a natural ability to find pattern in random form, as demonstrated by the Rorschach ink-blot test, and research by Philip Reeder suggests that certain forms on the map tend to be picked out consistently as zodiac material.[109] At least one well-documented zodiac has now been claimed by its author to be a conscious fabrication, and the astrologer John Addey has shown how easy it is to ascribe the characteristics of the signs of the zodiac to places chosen at random, in his humorous example of the Cheam Zodiac.[3]

It is now clear that terrestrial zodiacs are no more than a modern phenomenon, works of landscape art perhaps, or part of a growing movement towards perceiving quality and variety in the landscape. They are the product of our own imagination, but they can still provide a focus for pilgrimage, ritual or performance art[76] and can add significance to the interaction between an individual and the land.

BELOW *The Glastonbury Zodiac and The Girt Dog of Langport.*

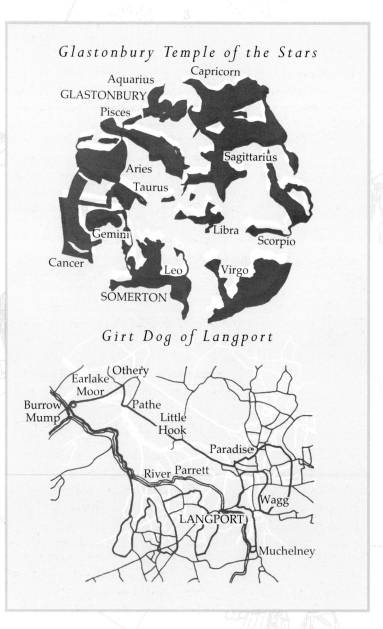

WIND AND WATER: THE PRACTICE OF FENG SHUI

Despite the findings of the Dragon Project and other workers over the years, it is still too early to be at all dogmatic as to the nature of the energies at ancient sites or how they might operate.

For a clue as to what might have been going on, we turn again to the Chinese system of *feng shui*, which was mentioned in Chapter 4.[43] *Feng shui* attempts to be aware of the flow of energies in the landscape, choosing the best sites, in terms of those energies, for the placing of a house, tomb, or other form of development. It also indicates ways in which the landscape can be modified in order to improve the flow of energies and thus the well-being of the inhabitants. John Michell points out:

Not that the early wandering people needed any formal system of feng shui, because, as they lived and moved under the direct influence of the earth's subtle energies, its principles were naturally integrated in their lives. Like all sciences, feng shui is an expedient of civilization, a technique for reconciling human nature to the limitations imposed on it by settlement.[93]

Having recognized that form is a reflection of the underlying energy pattern and that it interacts with it, it is possible for the best sites to be found. The ancient peoples were sensitive and could do this instinctively. In China, these sites were very quickly appropriated by the emperors and others who had power to take them. Others had to put up with less ideal locations, and this led to demand for the *feng shui* practitioner, whose skill was in improving the landscape by correct siting, ensuring that nothing took place to disturb the flows of energy. Stephen Skinner writes:

Conscious effort can correct the natural outlines of the Earth's surface to a more perfect configuration which will conserve and accumulate ch'i to the natural benefit of Earth, Man and Heaven...Ch'i is naturally accumulated and may be enhanced at certain points in the Earth by the application of landscape alterations made in accordance with feng shui rules.[117]

A whole range of landscape modifications began to be developed. The shape of a hill might be altered by the construction of earthworks, or even taking off a pointed peak. Mounds might be raised or pagodas built in a flat landscape or on a hilltop plateau. Trees might be planted or earthworks thrown up to the north of a house to disperse harmful *ch'i* emanating from that quarter. Ponds with gently flowing water and artificial waterfalls might be constructed or existing streams diverted to help the accumulaton of *ch'i*.

EARTH ENERGIES: A LIVING SYSTEM

A knowledge of *feng shui* enables us to look at some of the ancient sites elsewhere in the world in a new light. Were Watkins' mark points, the mounds, 'hill forts', moats and tree clumps, also the manifestation of some consciousness of the principles underlying the practice of *feng shui*? Very often stone circles and churches, for example, are on very good *feng shui* sites, as we have already noted with Castlerigg and Glastonbury Tor.

The altering of the landscape in order to achieve better energies at a site may be a simple matter, like tending a spring to make sure it continues to flow freely, or planting trees at a sacred spot. It may also involve more complex activity such as the construction of earthworks or artificial structures.

Just as water can be diverted by earthen banks for the purposes of drainage or irrigation, so many earthworks and structures may have had their origins in attempts to channel earth energies. Ian Taylor speculates:

Linear earthworks were the means of manipulating, channelling and containing vast flows of terrestrial energy, drawing them out of the central plateau area of the chalk uplands and leading them, sometimes for miles, towards places where they were required to boost the existing subtle currents.[120]

Legend suggests that many stones and springs have a healing power which could be encouraged by ritual. Such legends as the White Cow of Mitchell's Fold (see page 28) are a reminder, however, that this power can be misused and depleted.

Reichian therapy, acupuncture and many other healing techniques have as their basic principle the concept of energy flows in the body. The healing process involves correcting imbalances and freeing blockages, thus restoring a proper energy flow through the body (see chapter 4).

BELOW Glastonbury Tor, Somerset ,one of many examples of structures placed on prominent sites.

Acupuncture
~

Acupuncture, which originated in China, is the equivalent in many ways in the human body to *feng shui* in the landscape. It teaches that the human body is traversed by flows of *ch'i* along lines known as 'meridians'. At intervals along these are found acupuncture points which are stimulated by the insertion of needles, massage or warming with incense so as to balance the elements of *yin* and *yang* which make up the *ch'i,* an imbalance of which is thought to cause disharmony and disease. The flows of life energy in the body along the meridians are thus adjusted and balanced at certain very carefully chosen spots.

There seem to be strong parallels between energy in the body and energy in the landscape and, in the early 1970s, John Wheaton put forward in *The Ley Hunter* the idea of 'Earth Acupuncture'[139],

ABOVE *A modern acupuncturist treating a patient.*

subsequently taken up and developed by Tom Graves.[55] If the Earth is a living being its energy flows and sacred centres correspond to the meridians and acupuncture points in the human body. Therefore, the same sort of techniques as those of acupuncture might be used on the landscape to obtain equivalent results.

By analogy, the various rituals that take place at standing stones act like the acupuncturists' needles, encouraging and redistributing energy flows and freeing blockages. Beacon fires are a particularly vivid parallel with the technique of moxibustion, where small cones of moxa (*artemisia vulgaris*) are placed on the needles and lit. Recently, the sculptor, Marco Pogacnik has, with this in mind, installed stone sculptures in a German wood as an attempt at earth healing.

ENERGY DOWSING

Since the idea of earth energies was first put forward in the 1930s, attempts have been made to show that the ancient peoples could detect such energies and that, given the right conditions, we can do so today.

Much of the impetus behind such thinking has come from dowsers who realized that they were not just picking up underground water but something else, which they called telluric force. Bearing in mind the cautions given in Chapter 5, what have dowsers to tell us about ancient sites and earth energies?

Building on investigations by Reginald Allender Smith[118], who had detected what he felt were underground streams crossing beneath standing stones, Guy Underwood distinguished three types of dowsable line in the landscape: 'water-lines', 'track-lines' and 'aquastats'.

He thought that these were all 'lines of electrical equipotential' resulting from 'geophysical anomalies' and that ancient monuments, roads and boundaries coincided with them not by chance but because they were laid out by a priesthood who could detect the lines.[126]

Critics, while accepting the reality of the dowsable lines which Underwood had discovered, generally concluded that they were the result of the physical features rather than the reverse.

Underwood's somewhat arbitrary classification is now little used, but the patterns which he detected, multi-strand lines and spirals, continue to be found by those who in some cases have had little contact with his original work.

Bill Lewis spent many years dowsing the standing stones of his native South Wales and came to believe that a crossing of underground streams beneath each 'active' standing stone creates a small static electric field. The stone amplifies this and the energy emerges from the ground and up the stone in the form of a spiral having seven coils. He found the force varied and changed polarity with the lunar cycle.

Working independently, J. Havelock Fidler came up with original and valuable insights into the operation of earth energy. He found he could dowse the 'charge' in a stone, the wavelength being in the radio section of the electromagnetic spectrum, that this became fixed by electromagnetism, and that the germination of plants could be affected if they are on one of the 'charge lines'.[44]

Tom Graves could detect some form of 'charge' on standing stones and determine their polarity. There seemed to be fluctuations and cycles, from one of about 20 seconds to one corresponding to the monthly lunar cycle. He confirmed the findings of Underwood, who had noted a cycle which coincided with

the Celtic calendar, starting on the sixth day after the new and full moons. He also confirmed Lewis' findings, being able to detect seven bands on most large standing stones, and considered that these were 'tapping points into a spiral release of some kind of energy that moved up and down the stone, following the lunar cycle'.[55]

He considered that each band has specific properties. The fifth band affects a dowser's balance and throws them to one side: it is strongest at new and full moon. On touching the seventh band, the individual may feel that the stone is rocking or moving and feel a tingling sensation like a mild electric shock. It is also possible to release stored energy suddenly, resulting in a violent reflex contraction of the back muscles.

At Rollright circle, Graves was able to detect energy jumping from stone to stone. Where the line of stones breaks, lines of energy could be detected moving off at a tangent. On touching a certain stone, he appeared to release a massive pulse of energy as he acquired an instant migraine which lasted for 15 minutes. The pulses of energy

ABOVE *Energies experienced in standing stones seem to vary with the phase of the Moon. This is part of the alignment at Carnac in Brittany, France.*

released he called 'overgrounds'. They are dead straight and can be dowsed across country. They may correspond with leys.

American dowsers Terry Ross and Sig Lonegren found what they described as 'energy leys': these were also dead straight, could be dowsed, and might or might not correspond to an actual physical ley on the ground.[84]

For years dowsers have been detecting 'black streams' which may have been causing accidents or illness. More recently, 'energy leys' have been found which appear to have some of the same characteristics. By locating these and hammering stakes into the ground at strategic points, dowsers have been able to divert or stop the streams and return the house or area to a healthy state.

Caution in such activity is strongly urged as it can be very irresponsible to divert or alter energy flows without knowing what effect you may be having somewhere else.

RIGHT *The Cerne Abbas Giant, Dorset.*

BELOW *The power and gravitational pull of the moon effects the Earth's energy flows.*

A caution and a conclusion
~

In Chapter 5, I emphasised the dangers of reading too much into the results of dowsing. So often, we find what we want to find and this is particularly true when trying to dowse 'earth energies'. A whole edifice of alternative 'orthodoxy' has been built up on the most flimsy of foundations. Pure speculation is repeated endlessly and one ends up with a very confused picture. There are so many variables associated with dowsing for 'earth energies' that it would be most unwise to rely on it as a major source of information. The same with geomantic patterns in the countryside drawn on small-scale maps. It is fun to do, but there really are no large-scale geomantic patterns in the countryside that have any objective reality outside our own imaginings, if we are honest with ourselves. And terrestrial zodiacs are primarily works of art created by individuals themselves, perhaps helpful in relating to the landscape, but with no independent physical reality.

I do not intend this to be negative. It is rather that we need to clear away immature notions and concepts so that we can grow up and go forward, as I hope to show in the next chapter.

9

SHAMANIC LANDSCAPES

Earth Mysteries is a living subject – it is changing, developing, growing and maturing, continually moving towards a deeper appreciation of the true relationship between ancient peoples and the land they inhabited.

On a virtually non-existent budget, research work has been carried out over the past few years both in the landscape and with archive material, as well as, most significantly, forging cross-disciplinary links with other subjects.

The present chapter gives a broad outline of the direction in which the subject area has moved over the last few years. It is about a new way of looking at lines in the landscape and, indeed, the landscape itself. In the process, new insights have been obtained from sources as diverse as folklore, anthropology, consciousness studies and geophysics, which

subjects have also been enriched themselves as a result. Indeed it is with consciousness studies and a re-evaluation of folklore traditions that ancient landscapes have been seen with new eyes and a leap forward in Earth Mysteries has been accomplished.

But to take this path we must be prepared to grow, to realise that some concepts put forward in the heady days of the 1960s and 1970s, when the subject was young, can now be put to rest, as I indicated in the last chapter.

In order to progress and understand, it is vital to try and put ourselves in the position of those ancient peoples who were experiencing the landscape at first hand. Our task is to endeavour to enter their way of thinking and experiencing – to enter their consciousness.

THE MYSTERY LINES

As we saw in Chapter 2, linear landscape features occur throughout the world, from the lines of Nasca in Peru and the old Anasazi roads of Chaco Canyon to the prehistoric reaves, or field boundaries, and stone rows on Dartmoor, and the many examples now discovered by aerial photography of the Neolithic cursuses. They take different forms, but their essential characteristic – straightness – is clearly widespread. The number of instances of the straight landscape line now known throughout the world has multiplied and they have been found in so many different cultures that it begins to look as if we are dealing with some form of archetypal phenomenon.

It has become clear that what we are dealing with is not in any way one system. It is more that there is a repeated occurrence of

OPPOSITE Silbury Hill, in Wiltshire, is now recognized as the focus of an ancient sacred and symbolic landscape.

BELOW Archaic landscapes, such as this one at Nasca, Peru, are now beginning to be seen as an integrated whole.

straightness in the landscape because it comes from something very deep within the human being. As Paul Devereux makes clear:

'Watkins' term "ley" was… a generic term for archaic linear features of all kinds… Leys were never one particular type of feature, belonging to a specific culture and period of time.' [30]

Whatever it was that Watkins found was within a particular cultural context. He gives examples in his books of straight tracks and alignments in other parts of the world, and certainly in more recent times it has been realised that straightness in the landscape can emerge as a result of many different cultural stimuli. Whether such lines can be called 'leys' is really a relatively minor matter. Even Watkins dropped the term in the latter years of his life.

It is becoming clear that the straight line was such a universal feature, not just for the utilitarian reason that it was the shortest distance between two points, but for what it symbolised. It represented the unity of all existence, being the closest physical approximation to the deep spiritual link which transcends time and space. The straight line in the landscape was, in essence, a symbol of the reality of that Otherworld, where space was no barrier. It was the book from which universal truths were learned, particular teachings being imparted at specific places and times along the sacred tracks. [131]

LINES OF POWER

It is sometimes stated that linear landscape features are an example of the oppression of prehistoric society. [6] While straightness does exist in nature, for example the ray of sunlight, the waterfall, shadow and corn stalk, it is certainly true that it is often indicative of authority and domination. Jim Kimmis [74] has drawn attention to the root element 'reg', which can be found in many words meaning both straight and in authority, the word 'ruler', for example, having both meanings. Straight landscape lines could be, and undoubtedly sometimes were, used as an effective tool for political domination. The system of *ceques*, the straight tracks radiating out from the Temple of the Sun in the old Inca capital of Cuzco, is strong evidence for this.

A PASSAGE OF SPIRITS

In 1989, the editor of *The Ley Hunter*, Paul Devereux, achieved a breakthrough in understanding something of the purpose of archaic landscape lines, which allowed sense to be made of otherwise disparate material which had been around for some time. He published these revelations as the last chapter of his book *Lines on the Landscape*[105], which he wrote with Nigel Pennick. The unifying concept was that of the sanctity of the straight landscape line and its essential function as allowing the passage of the spirit.

The publication of this catalytic concept inspired others to look at some material in a new light and connections began to be made.

CORPSE WAYS

In Britain, corpse ways have been widespread. These are tracks, often straight, which led from outlying settlements to the churchyard and along which coffins were carried. There was an old belief in many places (which in fact has no legal credence) that to allow a coffin to be carried over one's land created a right of way. This seems to be an indication of the significance which was attached to these paths.

Devereux gives an example of a church way in Cornwall which led to the church of St Levan's. The track is marked by a small Celtic cross and, at the boundary of the churchyard, there is another old cross and a stone the size and shape of a coffin. [34]

DEATH ROADS

The first to respond was John Palmer in Holland. He found straight tracks, surviving from mediaeval times, focusing on cemeteries. Some of these, such as those north of Hilversum, still existed and went by the name of *doodwegen* or death roads. He began to make new connections between straightness in the landscape and death, and found mediaeval oaths revealing the importance which was placed on carrying an individual's corpse to the cemetery in a straight line along these roads. [32]

In Viking times, the bodies of chieftains were carried ceremonially to their burial ground along straight 'cult roads' such as that at Rosaring in Sweden, which is over 500 metres long and oriented exactly north-south.

GHOST PATHS

Ulrich Magin found what were known as *geisterwege* or ghost paths in Germany. These were associated with the spirits of the dead, or out-of-the-body spirits, nature spirits etc, and always ran in a straight line, ending at a cemetery. The spirits of the dead were believed to thrive on these paths. [88]

In Britain there are many examples of ghosts associated with paths leading to churchyards. Folklore researcher Jeremy Harte has found evidence in Dorset of such haunted paths, including particularly sightings of black dogs, which may have links with legends about the Wild Hunt, another manifestation of the ghost path. [61] The work of researchers into the alignment of black dog sightings in Devon takes on new significance in the light of this.

ABOVE *A simple Cornish cross which stands on the path betwen a farm and a church, two significant ley points.*

LEFT *Sightings of Black Dogs on ancient paths may have their origin in legends of the Wild Hunt.*

SPIRIT WAYS

Paul Devereux has suggested that the connecting link between death and ghosts can best be understood by seeing these paths as Spirit Ways.

❈

'We are looking at a spatial expression of a relationship with the dead – and, more precisely, with the ancestors. *That expression must have been based on some concept to do with the spirits of the dead, a concept, I suggest, that for some reason involves linking* spirits *with straightness. Dead straight.'* [32]

❈

Indeed, Watkins' 'leys' may in many cases be the vestiges of medieval spirit ways rather than prehistoric tracks, and the church alignments he found may, more accurately, be alignments of churchyards, although some of which, following research by Allen Meredith on the age of yew trees, are known to be older than the churches themselves.

This link between straightness and death can be traced back at least to Neolithic times with the cursuses – straight earthworks several miles long in some cases, frequently linked at one end to Long Barrows, which were used, at least in part, for burials.

THE SHAMANIC ORIGIN OF SPIRIT LINES

In his book '*Shamanism and the Mystery Lines*', Devereux states:

❈

'I became aware that the old 'core concept' was not only a connection between spirits and landscape lines, it was a deeper archaic complex that linked spirit movement with straight lines per se.'

'What I am suggesting, . . . is that this exceptionally ancient and now obscure association between spirit and straight linearity in 'ceremonial' landscapes is a common denominator that occurs, like the entopic images in rock art, because of the universality of the human central nervous system and its operation in shamanism.

The concept of the straight landscape line originates, I suggest, in a fundamental element of the shamanic experience, indeed, in what is arguably the central element of shamanism – magical flight. *This is simply a particular version of out-of-body experience.'* [32]

❈

What is being suggested here is something very fundamental which has wide implications. The ancient peoples were living far closer to nature than we are – they realized they were a *part* of nature. They could also enter 'altered states of consciousness' very much more easily than we can, using well-established shamanic techniques.

Certain individuals, known as *shamans* in Siberia, but known throughout the world by different names, could enter into this state – the shamanic trance – at will. It is while in this state that the shaman can undertake the ecstatic shamanic journey, which we know as an out-of-the-body experience. Also called astral projection, it is known in all cultures. Here, the spirit frequently transforms into an animal, leaves the body and appears to fly. In San (African bushman) shamanic trance, for example, the person 'transforms' into an antelope, and then leaves his or her body and flies. It is this flight of the soul that relates to the lines.

While there is some evidence that such flight is entopic, i.e. within the brain, perhaps linking neurologically with the near-death experience of a long straight tunnel or the UFO 'traction beam' frequently reported in abduction cases, there is also evidence that some flights may be actual ones over real landscape. I have experienced this for myself, and it seems to occur in a straight line over a recognized landscape. But ultimately whether this is physical or imaginary is actually not so important for the present purposes.

Devereux takes this a stage further: 'This shamanic flight of the soul seems to have been translated onto ancient sacred landscapes as straight lines. It seems to me that the lines are the symbolic representations of shamanic spirit journey routes: flight paths of the soul symbolically transferred to the solid earth.'[32]

This shamanic soul flight has much symbolism attached to it, particularly that of the bird, and phrases such as 'as the crow flies' and 'as straight as an arrow' are very much part of our language. Indeed, it may well be that one element in the unravelling of the straight landscape lines is that the straight line, being the shortest distance between two points, is thereby also the nearest thing in the physical world to that dissolution of distance which occurs in the state of being where the unity of all existence (sometimes known as 'cosmic consciousness') is experienced.

Awareness of these spirit lines across the landscape has been part of local tradition in many parts of the world. While the results of

this perceived or actual flight across the landscape could on occasions be seen in the landscape itself, such as the 'death roads' and corpse ways, at other times they seemed to be cultural concepts only. Particularly in Ireland, for example, fairy paths are common. These are straight paths which must be kept clear of any building as the fairies move along them. This has echoes in the Chinese practice of *feng shui* where similar strictures obtained. While not marked physically on the ground, they could be located geographically (i.e. people knew where they were).

Several other elements of folklore can now be reinterpreted as being linked with shamanic flight, such as the Wild Hunt which traditionally crossed the land at certain seasons in northern Europe. Even Santa Claus with his reindeer can be seen from this viewpoint.

ABOVE The Fairy Raid – Carrying off a Changeling, by Sir Joseph Noel Paton. The incursion of the 'Otherworld' is now often experienced as a UFO 'abduction'.

LEFT Father Christmas and his reindeer may well have their origin in the experience of shamanic flight.

WITCH WAYS

A vivid illustration of shamanic flight is
provided by the witch flying astride a
broomstick. Medieval witches made 'flying
ointments' which contained hallucinogenic
alkaloids. These were rubbed into the skin
and, in the altered state of consciousness thus
engendered, the witch could experience out-
of-the-body flight, often in the guise of some
animal such as a goose.[72]

There are traditions of witches following
particular paths. In Lincolnshire, for example,
Ethel Rudkin recounts the tale of a witch who
was flying from a temple above Anwick with
some stolen stones. She was shot at by some
shepherds and dropped the coffin-shaped
stones, which could still be seen at Ewerby
Waithe Common.[112] There is an alignment
between Dorrington Church, the Drake Stone
at Anwick and Ewerby Waithe Common.

THE MYTHOLOGISED LAND

Archaeologists are now beginning to realise
that ancient sites cannot just be looked at in
isolation. They are set in a landscape and their
relationship to that landscape and to each
other is highly significant.

People in ancient times related to the
landscape in which they lived to a far greater
extent than we can conceive. Indeed,
Devereux has referred to 'shamanic
landscapes', with the implication that the
whole of the landscape could be seen in this
way.[33] He quotes Levy-Bruhl, who refers to
the Marind people of Papua New Guinea:

*'... the native cannot look around him anywhere
without feeling in a very vivid way that here, there
and everywhere some supernatural power, some
mythic being, has at some time made his presence
felt, and indeed may still be present in the place.
Earth and sea are to him as living books in which
the myths are inscribed ... a legend is captured in
the very outlines of the landscape.'* [82]

This is perhaps most clearly shown by the
Australian aborigines, who see the topography
as being formed by the Dreamings who
emerged from the earth. The paths they took,
which were followed during seasonal
ceremonial journeys, were sanctified, and
sacred sites each had their appropriate songs
and rituals which had to be performed. These
sites might be boulders, caves, a heap of
stones or a pavement of white quartz. It
becomes clear that the outer landscape and
the inner landscape are, for the aborigines, a
unity and that one can only be understood by
reference to the other.

In his book *Symbolic Landscapes*, Devereux
has tried to approach the Avebury area from a
similar viewpoint, showing how the
relationships between the different elements
that make up that sacred landscape – Silbury
Hill, West Kennet Long Barrow, Windmill
Hill and the great stone circle itself all relate
to the surrounding landscape in a striking way
if looked at with the right eyes.[33]

10

HOMES
OF THE
EARTH SPIRIT

For me, the study of Earth Mysteries covers
far more than some long-forgotten people and
the monuments they left: it is firmly rooted
in the present and in our own relationship to
the Earth.

Perhaps it is inevitable, when looking at
prehistoric sites, that attention has
concentrated on artificial constructions,
particularly dramatic ones like stone circles.
Yet, particularly as the early Christians

accused the pagans of worshipping trees and
streams and stones, it seems likely that it was
the natural sites which were looked upon as
being truly important.

In this chapter, I want to examine some sites
which hold a particular attraction for me and,
remembering Allen Watkins' account of how
his father has classified sites according to the
four elements, I have chosen representatives
of three of these – earth, water and air.

THE LIVING ROCK

Stone was important to the ancient people, from the siting of humble markstones to the erection of massive stone circles.

The type of stone seemed to matter, since in many cases the nearest source was eschewed in favour of more distant origins, the most famous case being the bluestones of Stonehenge, brought 200 miles (300km) from the Preseli Mountains in Wales.

We are only beginning to realize the significance of stone. Dragon Project researcher, Don Robins, has shown that stone has a 'defect structure', which means that it has gaps which can trap electrons. Free electrons can therefore flow in from the atmosphere and the earth, thus producing electrical phenomena. Electrons can also be released by the application of energy.[111] This all shows that stones are very active and can absorb and give out energies. Indeed, a whole body of knowledge has grown up around the uses of different types of crystal in healing and meditation, and we have seen from folklore that ancient people attributed value and properties to certain stones.

As a counterpoint to the dramatic formation of major fault lines and tectonic intrusions, which are major focuses for the occurrence of earth lights phenomena, the slow deposition of sedimentary rocks builds up the character of an area in its own way. Character, which is

ABOVE *Carn Meini, Preseli Hills, Wales, where it is thought the original bluestones of Stonehenge came from.*

❧

OPPOSITE *The depiction of the four elements has beguiled many great artists. This is Earth by Jan Breughel (1568–1625).*

❧

BELOW *Chalk landscape with wooded valleys and open uplands has always attracted those who are sensitive to the earth spirit.*

what geography is about, depends, at root, on the underlying rock. If each of the rock strata had their own 'morphogenetic field', to use Sheldrake's term, or 'landscape deva', to use different terminology, might we not be able to detect these as different 'psychic atmospheres'?

To take the example of chalk, some of the most memorable days of my childhood were spent cycling in the North Downs in Surrey. Pushing my bike up those long hills and dry valleys gave me an intimate understanding of the nature of the chalk landscape. I find it difficult to put my thoughts and feelings about this into words, so I will leave it to others.

The occultist, Dion Fortune, wrote that 'the best place to wake the old gods is on chalk!'.[47] Comedian Michael Bentine recounted that he had asked a sensitive why some part of the chalk countryside around Folkestone, where he lived, gave him a great feeling of security and peace while others made him feel uncomfortable and nervous. The answer received was that all people who have lived in that area have imprinted their personalities on the chalk, which in origin is organic, and that he was picking this up: 'As a sensitive, you *replay*, like a gramophone record, everything that has been recorded on the chalk. Even the shape and form of the Downs – often moulded and cut by man – affects you.'[4]

Magical Chalk Pits
~

Anyone of a moderately sensitive disposition, who is not in the thrall of what Aldous Huxley termed their 'idiot monologue' of petty rigmarole, but who is sufficiently inwardly tranquil and open to the influence of the landscape, cannot fail to be struck by the uncanny quality which the chalk 'breathes out' at different times of day under particular atmospheric conditions. When the weather has entered a relatively rain free period, but when cloud cover is moderately dense and uniform, but not too low – when the prevailing light is evenly spread over the landscape, with no parts over bright or too deep in shadow – when the wind is still or gently fitful, a magic prevails everywhere upon the Wolds, and it comes from within the chalk. When the above conditions obtain, at dusk or dawn, mid-morning or afternoon, it is the same. I have encountered it so often in a lengthy acquaintance with this landscape, I know it as well as my own name. It is the essential inner spirit of the earth here – immemorial and profoundly mystical – and nowhere is it so potent as upon the edges of these curious chalk pits.

Every time I visit a relatively unspoilt pit I step into this magic. As with dew ponds and tumuli the edges of chalk pits are the places of greatest power (and the points where the leys pass). If you sit for long enough you can feel the energy swirling around the rim. In the bottom of the pit there is a corresponding calm – it is the still centre of the spiral – and an odd sense of hollowness, as if you were about to drop into the deeps of the earth's psyche (and of your own) like a stone down a mineshaft. This emotional response seems to be the result of the unique *yin*-formation of the pit: deep unconscious imagery can arise in these places, and a mood of chastening solemnity will prevail.[120]

IAN TAYLOR,
The All-Saints Ley Hunt.

It seems important and fruitful to develop the link with the very rock beneath us. Itzhak Bentov envisages the example of a cleft in a rock where animals can find refuge. Birds start to nest there and, gradually, consciousness evolves into a 'spirit of the rock'. People begin to become aware of this embryonic spirit, and their thoughts and feelings gradually enable it to build up into a powerful tribal god.[5]

Kaledon Naddair, the researcher and writer on Keltic tradition and prehistoric rock art, has told how, in searching for new examples of rock carvings, he has attempted to contact rock spirits – actual spiritual beings that inhabit sites. They are alive, can come out of the rock and can materialize. He feels that it is because he has a high ethical and moral standard in his approach to sacred sites that he has earned their trust over the years. He can now make contact with the rock spirits in a friendly and positive manner, being guided to new cup-and-ring marks, some hidden 6in (15cm) below the turf.[99]

BELOW *The pit has a spiritual as well as a purely utilitarian dimension.*

ABOVE *The
Externsteine, near
Padeborn, has long been
one of Germany's most
sacred sites.*

Rock climbers can become very aware of the living nature of their element. Jim Perrin, interviewing the climber John Gill, refers to how some hypnagogic states have their parallels in situations of action and describes how, on easy routes, Gill 'could feel himself weaving in and out of the rock, peering out from the other side of its surface'.[106]

There is some suggestion that psychic communication can flow more easily along strata than across them and a true link can thus be formed through the Earth between those sites on similar strata. All those who visit springs on the chalk are thereby linked with others doing the same. This is admittedly mere speculation, but it does suggest an interesting line in telepathy experiments.

Before the days of intensive quarrying, natural rock outcrops were of great significance. Many folktales relate to natural outcrops, which are often, like Uluru (Ayers Rock) in Australia and Externsteine in Germany, the most sacred of sites. If natural rock is such an influence and repository of

psychic memory, it is not surprising that the sites where it outcrops to the surface should be considered so special.

The largest rock outcrop in the whole of the East Riding of Yorkshire, apart from coastal cliffs, is a deposit of breccia known as Drewton Pillar. It is also called St Austin's Stone, because of the legend that St Augustine (also known as 'Austin') preached from it and baptized converts in the spring below. This seems to indicate that the rock was of sacred significance a long time before Augustine came to England to preach. This is more obviously the case with the Devil's Pulpit, at Tealby, Lincolnshire, which is a natural rock outcrop with the tradition of being a witches' meeting place.

Natural 'amphitheatres' have a powerful effect: the tallest waterfall in England, Hardraw Force, near Hawes, Yorkshire, is very impressive, the waterfall itself not being visible until one enters the circular amphitheatre. Such places – places where one can get close to the earth spirit – would have been very special to ancient peoples.

SPRINGS AND HOLY WELLS

OPPOSITE *The living element of water depicted by Jan Breughel (1568–1625).*

OPPOSITE BELOW *Lud's Well, Stainton-le-Vale, Lincolnshire.*

RIGHT *Cloutie Well, Munlochy, Ross and Cromarty: rags were commonly left as offerings at holy wells.*

BELOW *St Helen's Well, Goodmanham, East Yorkshire. Pure water flows straight out of the hillside into this pool.*

Holy wells are defined by Edna Whelan and Ian Taylor as naturally occurring springs, only slightly modified by human hand.[140] They have the characteristic of never running dry in the longest drought or freezing in the coldest frost. They may be prehistoric, dedicated to the Goddess Brighde and Diana; some have been Christianized, such as the many St Helen's Wells.

Some are simple springs issuing from a hillside. Others flow into a stone tank or pond, or have a brick well-housing, with steps leading down to the water. There is often an intimate association between a holy well and trees growing nearby or directly above. These are frequently hawthorn or elder.

In these days of piped water supply, it is difficult to appreciate the significance and importance of sources of pure water. Perhaps with concern growing about contaminants and residues in our drinking water, the holy wells may come into their own again, although many have dried up through the permanent lowering of the water table.

Holy wells also had other, more esoteric, functions, such as healing. It was the custom to tear a piece of rag from a garment, take it out to the holy well before dawn, soak it in the water and tie it to a nearby tree as an offering. This practice still occurs in places. Some were described as pin wells where, in a similar fashion, a pin was dropped into the well and a wish was made. These healing properties were often fairly specific, covering a wide range of ailments but particularly connected with sore eyes. Sufferers were prepared to travel considerable distances to use such waters. The healing function might be allied to homeopathy, where very small changes in the chemical composition of the water could have very specific curative effects.

The presence of earth energies adds another dimension. Phenomena are frequently reported at springs and streams, as Lethbridge noted and as we have seen in the context of visions of fairies and the Virgin Mary. A sleepy

state may be induced, as Devereux reports of the holy well at Sancreed in Cornwall, where almost an entire group of 15 people became languid or fell asleep. He also has this to say:

❦

Old holy wells and springs are traditional interfaces with the Earth spirit, and this can usually be almost palpably felt at such places; they are truly sacred locations. It would be a gross violation to carry out noisy or even physically energetic rituals or ceremonial activities at them. Dreaming is ideal for such sites; if the dreams of Earth can be dreamt anywhere, it is at these sacred waters. Drink the water at the spring or well, then curl up and go to sleep near the point of issue, after invoking the anima mundi. *At these sites more than anywhere else it is appropriate to visualize the Earth spirit as a goddess figure, because, as J.C. Cooper observes, sacred waters are traditionally 'symbolic of the Great Mother, and associated with birth, the feminine principle, the universal womb, the* prima materia, *the waters of fertility and refreshment and the fountain of life'.*[24]

❦

Lud's Well, Stainton-le-Vale
~

A steep scramble down an ivy-covered slope leads one into a place of great natural beauty alive with the earth spirit force. Luxuriant and massive fern ground cover, the visual and aural beauty of the undocumented sacred waters cascading over small waterfalls, contribute to a truly magical atmosphere, a positive retreat from the world above.

The most sensorily significant of the two springs is the one which emerges from the northern hillside. Reaching back into the womblike darkness of Mother Earth the waters issue forth into a small pool, then over an edge being transformed into a miniature cascade.[38]

BOB DICKINSON

TREES AND SACRED GROVES

Trees are representatives of the air element in the landscape. They come out of the earth, but they dwell in the air. Each leaf makes contact with the air, and anyone who has been in a grove of beech trees on a windy night can have no doubt as to the elemental attribution of the tree.

Trees and tree clumps have a special attraction for me as they symbolized my own introduction to Earth Mysteries, through Tony Wedd. He read *The Old Straight Track* in 1949 when living in London and, fresh from reading, he took a walk across Parliament Hill to Highgate Ponds:

…turning there towards Ken Wood, and climbing up the slope, I spotted a solitary Scots pine tree among the beeches. 'A mark!' I called ecstatically. It stood a clear 10ft above the other trees, like a flag on top of a fortress, its mushroom structure always pressing for the extra light due to its extra height.

It often seems to me that the lay of the land itself reveals the angle from which a mark is meant to be approached. So, as I stood there on Hampstead Heath, I felt that it was just from that point of view that the single surviving Pinus sylvestris *was intended to be seen. With what delight, therefore, on scanning the surrounding heath did I spot, barely 50 yards to my left — The Tumulus! There is only the one, topped by* Pinus sylvestris, *and encircled by a crown of thorns.*[135]

Plotting the line on a map, he found that it passed straight through Westminster Abbey, the site of which was originally known as Thorney Island from a conscpicuous mark: a hallowed clump of hawthorn. He began to speculate that the ley was marked with hawthorns on the lower ground, pines on the higher ground, and that the double planting around the tumulus was to mark the changeover.

On moving to Kent, Wedd began to explore the countryside and kept coming across tree clumps occupying prominent positions on or near hilltops. From his flat at Chiddingstone Castle, which offered good views out to the north and east, he noticed a clump of pines breaking the skyline. They drew the eye to One Tree Hill, now forested over, and from this clump, at Chested, he could look back over the top of Chiddingstone Castle to another clump at Mark Beech beyond. He later extended the line in both directions and continued to plot and photograph tree clumps in the surrounding countryside, gradually discovering several more alignments, including a parallel system extending from the Sevenoaks Range to the High Weald in Sussex. This seemed to confirm Watkins' findings in Herefordshire and the Welsh border of the particular significance of Scots pine as a ley mark point.[134]

Largely as a result of Wedd's enthusiasm, I found myself becoming irresistibly attracted to the Scots pine — the solitary tree as well as the clump — not just as a potential ley mark point, but as something in its own right. I was not alone: legend seems to confirm the special nature of the pine.

BELOW *The power and magic that emanates from a grove of ancient trees is almost palpable; many people who become interested in Earth Mysteries are first attracted by trees.*

Frazer refers to the pine becoming an object of worship during the orgiastic festival of Cybele and Attis in Rome each spring equinox. He describes how, in another ceremony, an image of Osiris was buried in the hollowed-out centre of a pine tree. As he says: 'It is hard to imagine how the conception of a tree as tenanted by a personal being could be more plainly expressed.'[49]

The pine was particularly sacred to Dionysus. A wand tipped with a pine cone was commonly carried by the god or his worshippers. The pine cone appeared on many ancient amulets and was regarded as a symbol of fertility.

Mirov and Hasbrouck mention that pines were also considered sacred in Mexico and Central America, where the incense-fragrant rosin of the 'pine of the gods' was burnt as an offering in the temples. They add:

The Buriats, a Mongolian people living around the southern end of Lake Baikal in East Siberia, often viewed Scots pine groves as sacred. These 'shaman forests' were scattered over dry grassland. Before the Soviet revolution of 1917, one approached and rode through the groves in silence lest the gods and spirits of the woods be offended.[96]

Galleons Lap
~

They walked on, thinking of This and That, and by-and-by they came to an enchanted place on the very top of the Forest called Galleons Lap, which is sixty-something trees in a circle; and Christopher Robin knew that it was enchanted because nobody had ever been able to count whether it was sixty-three or sixty-four, not even when he tied a piece of string round each tree after he had counted it. Being enchanted, its floor was not like the floor of the Forest, gorse and bracken and heather, but close-set grass, quiet and smooth and green. It was the only place in the Forest where you could sit down carelessly, without getting up again almost at once and looking for somewhere else. Sitting there they could see the whole world spread out until it reached the sky, and whatever there was all the world over was with them in Galleons Lap.[95]

A.A. MILNE,
The House at Pooh Corner.

I believe the Druid sacred groves to have been functionally identical with, and a direct continuity of, ley mark-clumps. Tony Wedd discovered clumps in Wiltshire and Somerset which he thought were the remains of sacred groves, based on the presence of most of the trees described by Robert Graves as forming the Celtic tree alphabet and tree calendar, and which may be a significant guide to the presence of a grove.[54.]

Continuing survival becomes more likely when we consider the practice which I have described as 'tending'. Consciously or unconsciously, the trees, either individually or in clumps, are recognized by local people as being sacred, and they are given a helping hand to ensure their survival. This was done, on certain occasions by deliberate ritual, to maintain the subtle energies at a site as well as the physical features. Most work was very modest, keeping the right trees and plants growing well and excluding the others – in other words, weeding.

ABOVE *Oil from
the sweet almond
(Prunus dulcis) has
many medical and
cosmetic uses; it helps to
relieve muscular pains
and encourages soft,
supple skin.*

It is this tradition which I suspect has been handed down over the generations in particular families, but which is dying out. Our particular role may be to take over consciously and with some degree of awareness that which was formerly done on a more instinctive level. And we had better do it quickly, because the trees and clumps are rapidly disappearing through the ravages of storms and neglect.

There may have been a body of people, in medieval or even later times, who, either quite consciously or otherwise, planted clumps or individual trees in the 'right' spots. But there may also be another process which helps to keep the trees and the clumps in good heart. The sites where tree clumps now exist may have particular etheric qualities which encourage the growth of particular species or groups of species, so the natural and created landscape gradually takes on the form of the underlying pattern of energies. The clumps and individual trees we see today may only have been planted in the eighteenth and nineteenth centuries as part of the general landscape revival, on the apparent whim of an individual farmer, but some clumps may have survived better than others because the energies were right, and this may have enabled some of them to have had a continued existence from more distant times.

ABOVE *Oil from the
herb aniseed (Pimpinella
anisum) is a basis for
folk remedies for coughs
and bronchitis.*

There seems to be an energy spirit in each tree and each species which can be seen by sensitives. These seem identical to Sheldrake's morphogenetic fields and to what the ancient Sanskrit texts refer to as a *deva* (or 'shining one'). This latter term is used by the sensitive, Dorothy Maclean, of the Findhorn Community, Scotland. She found that she could tune in to the nature spirits and *devas* overlighting particular species and areas of landscape. The detailed instructions which were obtained were followed, and the famous garden flourished in the sand dunes as a direct result of this collaboration.[87]

ABOVE RIGHT
*Wherever they grow,
pine trees have an effect
on people who walk
among them.*

The Theosophists claim that a grove of mature trees has an energy pattern which assists in the raising of consciousness, and, in this context, with particular respect to pines, Mirov and Hasbrouck write:

Poets also shared in describing the beauty of pines… All of us get elated and emotional as we stroll through a pine grove on a hot summer day when the old trees fill the air with their pungent fragrance. Big bonfires made of pitchy pinewood have a peculiar mystic fascination. As we sit watching the sparks going up, and as we inhale the fragrant smoke, we are inclined to become philosophical or to sing nostalgic songs… Longfellow wrote beautifully of 'Piny odours in the night air'. We are all poets when we are in the pine woods.[96]

Dion Fortune describes the Fire of Azrael, consisting of sandalwood, juniper and cedar, the scent from which is said to aid clairvoyance.[48] Many are uplifted by the scent of pines. Paul Baines has shown that this is caused by the essential or volatile oils, which the alchemists considered to be the soul of a plant.[68] It appears that the scent of these oils can affect the etheric body, perhaps creating the right atmosphere for particular states of consciousness, and ancient peoples may have been aware of this. Such techniques as aromatherapy seem to operate similarly, and the use of incense to achieve specific effects in meditation and ritual is well established.

Aromatherapy
~

Aromatherapy may be defined as the use of the natural scents and essential oils from a variety of trees, shrubs and flowers for assistance in the healing of dis-ease in the individual. Scott Cunningham has developed the practice of magical aromatherapy, where he uses these natural aromas for effects such as stimulation of the mind, protection, purification and psychic awareness, thereby attaining what might be called magical states of consciousness.[21]

Thus 'etheric geography' opens up another possibility of interpreting the landscape in a more subtle and complete way than has usually been done. And with the help of naturalists and ecologists (and some of the best are very much aware of these added dimensions to their subjects) it becomes possible to do consciously what has so far remained in the instinctive realm.

The effect which pines and other trees have on the emotions of those who visit them is formalized in the work of Dr Edward Bach, who developed a series of remedies, based on plant extracts, which work directly on the mental or emotional state of the person.[137]

Havelock Fidler, the dowser, found that the Scots pine acted as an 'interruptor' of energy lines,[44] and Paul Baines speculates that the trees may thus be capable of drawing and absorbing the energy pattern of disease from those who need treatment or adjustment.[68]

Perhaps in ancient times people had to go out into the landscape to find their healing rather than bringing the remedy to the person, and we may again find healing in the landscape by tending and restoring old clumps.

Ian Taylor speculates that tree clumps may act as a respiratory system, drawing up earth energies and releasing them through the clump's composite aura, as well as performing the same function with subtle celestial stimuli. Seeing a parallel in Reich's work with the human body, he links the health of the tree clumps with the free energy flow of the Earth,

any blockages being manifested in disease. Conversely, the health of the tree clump could be transmitted out to the surrounding landscape, having the function of the kidneys in the body.[109]

All this is an integrative vision – linking our health and state of being with that of the landscape itself. It points us towards the reasons for visiting ancient sites: each has its own unique atmosphere which we can literally take into our very being.

Perhaps it is not too late, by some sort of active 'tending', to re-create the atmospheres of ancient sites by reintroducing plants which may once have been there, so that they can again contribute their specific fragrance, their own note which helps create the ethereal music of the place. And these will be living places, whose character will change with the cycle of the seasons. The skills of the aromatherapist and the incense blender can combine with those of the landscape architect and conservation volunteer to create once again sacred groves for specific magical and healing purposes.

ABOVE *The essential oil from Cubebs (Piper cubeba), a member of the pepper family, is used for medicinal, cosmetic and culinary purposes. It is particularly useful for respiratory and digestive complaints.*

ABOVE *Essential oil from nutmeg (Myristica fragrans) is used to treat the circulatory, digestive and nervous system.*

TOP LEFT *Flowers from the forget-me-not family (Boraginaceae), including comfrey, lungwort, borage, hound's tongue and bugloss, all of which have a place in the repertoire of folk remedies.*

11

LISTENING
TO THE
EARTH

I wrote the following lines several years ago about a site which I visit regularly as an indication of the sort of way in which we might best approach sacred sites in the landscape.

❧

I leave the motor road high up on the open Wolds, and take the chalk and flint surfaced green lane. The woods crowd in on me as I make my way along the ancient track. The energy paths of every being which literally made their way along here before me have permeated the very fabric of the earth and my footsteps are well guided indeed.

I pause a moment beside an ancient grove of beech trees, tended no longer now, though their presence and calm remain. Here, perhaps, within living memory, the ancient rites were enacted and may yet be again. The trees will stay in readiness for that time. At the top of the dry valley I scramble down to the green path, following the old hedge of thorns and elders, pointing the way, beckoning me onwards as I descend the gently curving path down the rolling hillside.

*The hill edges in more closely. Instinctively
I take off my shoes and feel the springy grass
beneath my bare feet. Past more bushes now, I stand
for a moment on the edge of a sacred area, which I
share with the rabbits for which it is home. I am
also conscious of a silent harmony with all those –
past and to come – who have touched the beauty
and inspiration of this place.*

*Onwards now and down the narrow sloping
path under the hillside trees, down, scrambling to
the valley bottom; then, turning back, to make the
last gentle descent to the small chalk cliff. I kneel
down and drink from the renewing,
strengthening, sacred spring.*

*All is silent – the sun is set and as the branches of
the woodland trees reflect in the gentle water of the
pool I feel the whole of existence draw closer around
me as my capacity for description dissolves into an
experience of the infinite.*[65]

My own belief is that Earth Mysteries
should be relevant to the present day, and that
means we must make our own relationship
with the sacred sites. To be involved in Earth
Mysteries is much more than just reading in
an armchair or researching in the library: it
means going out and becoming part of the
landscape ourselves.

The landscape – the Earth and her sites – are
our finest teachers, if we can but allow them
to be so. One of our problems is that most of
us live in towns. Indeed, as Paul Devereux
once said 'Even if we live in the countryside,
we're still a load of townies'. In other words,
it's a question of attitude as much as location.
We have divorced ourselves from the
landscape and the countryside and one of the
implications of this is that we are apt to see
our visits to ancient sites from the perspective
of the tourist – as a spectacle.

While that may be interesting (and I am not
suggesting that we should refrain totally from
such activity), something more is needed if we
are really to approach the Earth and the earth
spirit with any depth and with any hope of
useful results.

Firstly, we must be clear what our aim is. I
suggest that what we are really trying to do is
to re-establish contact with the earth spirit
through visiting sites, to emphasize pilgrimage

rather than tourism. So, forget for the
moment the big tourist attraction: explore
your local area. The sites may not be so
dramatic, but you will be surprised at what
you discover if you aim really to get to know a
particular area. The sites may sometimes be
hidden and need to be sought out, and this can
only happen by taking time and effort.

Sites vary throughout the world, and it is
important to look at the local situation. My
examples tend to come from the part of the
world where I live, but the same principles
apply wherever you happen to be. There are
always sacred sites which you can find if you
attune to the spirit of the area and keep your
senses alert.

You may find a forgotten holy well or
markstone, or the remnants of a tree clump in
a neglected corner. Just wander round,
keeping to the public footpaths and tracks,
seeing where you end up. You will find sites
and you will discover the right ways to
approach them as well.

ABOVE *The
atmosphere created by a
clump of Scots Pines is
often magical.*

OPPOSITE *Springs
on the edge of the
Yorkshire Wolds.*

Visit the area several times and you will find yourself being attracted to a few sites in particular: these are the places where you can meet the earth spirit. Just allow your intuitive faculties to operate, open your heart and be honest with yourself and the landscape.

This is what Paul Devereux has called 'being and seeing'. This involves going to a site with no instrumentation of any sort, no dowsing rods, camera, Geiger counter or even pencil. Not even any ideas. Just go and allow yourself to be taught by the site. The site will reveal itself as a living teacher.[28]

But first you must ask permission of the spirit of the site, even if you are not directly conscious of such a being. Then you must give. If the site is neglected, you should re-establish the practice of tending. This may involve clearing out the clogged-up holy well, weeding round the markstone so that it can be seen, or encouraging the old tree species and companion plants where a clump is threatened. Even picking up litter on a regular basis is a positive, life-affirming act.

You will realize by such actions that you have 'adopted' the site and, if you act rightly, honestly, and with good intentions, it will thank you. In its own way, the site will respond by allowing you to share in its store of wisdom. A two-way process of healing will have been initiated.

You can develop the link further by visiting regularly, at different times of the day, such as dawn, noon, sunset and midnight, at times of the full moon, perhaps, or the eight traditional festivals. Whether you wish to perform any ritual is up to your natural inclination, but you will learn the ways of the earth spirit in a manner that you could never learn in books.

The important thing is to be open to the place: let it speak to you until you become aware of its spiritual essence. Then make that place special to you by conducting a ritual, in whatever form you feel happiest with. It is best for you to follow your instincts and make up your own ritual. Certainly such things that you may already have done, such as approaching the site along the right sacred path and clearing litter are valid rituals in their

own right. The important thing is that they should be non-invasive: in other words, play music rather than leave crystals. Treat the site with respect. Don't try and change things, at least until you understand them, and that may take a lifetime, at least.

Nigel Pennick refers to the ancient practice of 'sitting out', where a persons its in the open at night in a meditative state, at high places of ancient sanctity, and solitary wild place of power. It may also involve a physical pilgrimage along ancient sacred paths, or wandering a wild area until one finds a good place for 'sitting out'.[104]

I don't mean to suggest that such things as scientific monitoring or the use of dowsing rods are inappropriate at ancient sites: rather that we should as far as possible leave our preconceptions behind as we approach and allow the site if it wishes, to speak to us. And that takes time. It's easy enough to say this: I know from experience how difficult it is in practice!

The aim is to balance the left and right hemispheres of the brain – the analytical and the intuitive – using both in tandem. This is difficult as we are not used to doing it, preferring to keep these approaches in separate compartments. We have to learn new techniques to integrate them.

One approach to sites is to look at the way we experience them through our senses. In the Zen and Taoist traditions, it was always

the aim to get beyond words to the direct experience, and an emphasis on the senses rather than the thoughts may be a help in achieving this very necessary state.

Jimmy Goddard has made a creative leap in linking the sites corresponding to the elements through the medium of sound. On visiting Gill's Lap pine clump, it seemed to him that the sound of the wind in the trees was very similar to the sound of a rushing stream and also to that of a roaring fire. On experimenting, he found that they were all within the frequency range of 256 to 320 cycles per second, and speculated that such sounds were capable of being transduced to boost the earth current. I feel that they may also have been used to help induce altered states of consciousness.[68] Bob Dickinson adds another dimension:

Many a time I have walked in the neighbouring church grounds aurally locating the sound of the distant well [Ashwell], shifting my focus to the sound of the wind blowing through the tops of an adjacent circle of Scots Pine, then merging the two together in a synthesis of natural sound to create a powerful aurally based sense of place.[37]

He also draws attention to the power of natural forces to produce sound in the landscape such as the 'death songs' caused by a reed vibrating in the wind.[40] We may be reminded of the 'hummadruz', or mysterious humming with no apparent cause, which occurs from time to time, particularly at ancient sites. A friend of mine recalls an occasion in her childhood, as she was walking along an ancient path, when she heard the sound of thunder from the ground: none of the friends she was with heard anything.

We use the sense of sight all the time. Sir George Trevelyan proposes that our seeing should be an active deed rather than a passive reception of images. This is in no way contradictory to the principle of allowing a site to speak to us, but illumines a different aspect of our experience. He puts forward the concept of the 'eye-beam', as an instrument of perception with which we can actually touch and feel objects:

The difference between this and our normal looking may seem small but it is fundamental, since the mental attitude of recognizing the active deed of directing a finger of looking to touch the building is experienced as a real extension of consciousness far beyond the limits of the physical body.[123]

We have already noted the sense of smell in our examination of the effect of the subtle essences and perfumes which emanate from the trees and herbs at a site. The sense of touch is also a very fundamental one in that it is easier to get beyond the barrier of words and thoughts to direct experience this way. We can, at the very least, as I suggested in the opening passage, approach a site barefoot, making a direct link with the Earth. Better still, if the site is sufficiently isolated, we can remove our clothes completely (or go 'skyclad', as the witches say). We can again feel the wind, the warmth and the cold on our body, which is a new experience for many and does, in some strange way, draw one closer to Nature for that reason alone. We can touch the site, embrace the trees and stones. It is not too fanciful to say that they need to be loved and welcome our presence.

There can be no precise directions on how to approach sites. All we can do is to follow our inner guidance, realize we are a part of the Earth, and we will know.

BELOW *Cole's Tump, Herefordshire – Tony Wedd helped to revive interest in these landscape features*

12

TOWARDS
AN
INTEGRATION

This book began with the image of the Earth as seen from space and the changes of consciousness which accompanied this vivid symbol of the holistic vision. Earth Mysteries study is part of this vision and has its own role in helping show us how we fit into the whole picture.

We started with the old straight track, leading us along the old ways into the heart of the countryside, right to the spots the ancient people held specially sacred. Along the way, we heard folk tales about these places — memories of stones that glowed and springs that healed and rituals performed. We learnt that from ancient times people had been aware of an energy in living things and in the landscape, of modern attempts to learn about it, and of the growing recognition that it was truly the life energy of the earth goddess, Gaia. Finally, we looked at ways in which, by visiting the places of ancient power, we can again attune ourselves to her presence. This is the essence of Earth Mysteries: not mystery for its own sake but a recognition of the depths of experience which can occur at these ancient sites, places where contact with the living Earth at all her levels can again be made and where we can feel part of her.

One way of looking at Earth Mysteries is as a set of interlocking themes concerned with our relationship to the Earth and the way people have experienced her subtle body through the medium of energies in the landscape.

THE LIFE ENERGY OF GAIA

The theme of energy has been one of the strongest threads running through from ancient legends to the last Dragon Project research. Its reality is undeniable, but its nature is unclear: whether it consists merely of known forces in unfamiliar contexts or the manifestation of something more fundamental which has been recognized by psychics and mystics throughout history, is open to interpretation.

What seems increasingly clear is that the energy felt at ancient sites is a manifestation of the subtle body of Gaia – the earth goddess. The recognition of the Earth as a living being is central to Earth Mysteries, which aims to explore the implications of this fact, both at the higher levels of consciousness and at the level of day-to-day existence. In this it has links with both ecological and spiritual movements.

With the perceived energies coursing through her aura, Gaia is infinitely more complex, subtle and wise than we are, as mere human beings. All the evidence, from modern researchers such as Rupert Sheldrake to the most ancient religious cosmology, unwaveringly suggests that living beings exist on levels other than the physical and, indeed, that our definition of 'living' may have to be expanded to include such apparently inanimate things as rock.

ABOVE *An abstract rendition of Gaia, the spirit of the earth, generally considered to be female.*

OPPOSITE *Caer Caradoc, Church Stretton, Shropshire.*

PAGANISM

Paganism exists today in many forms, including witchcraft. Witches still visit ancient sites to attune to Gaia in her various manifestations and, along with many other modern pagan groups and individuals, thereby gain wholeness and peace.

At the simplest level, we can, as individuals or small groups, follow ancient paths to magical places in the depths of the country at special times and, leaving behind our preconceived notions, experience such sites in an open way, allowing the energies to manifest within us.

Paganism has the characteristics of what Joseph Campbell has called 'Type I' religions. These include an acknowledgement that creation in the universe is a continuous process; that time is cyclical rather than linear; that there is no boundary between the self and the non-self (in contrast to what Alan Watts[123] called 'the skin-encapsulated ego'); that there is more than one 'reality'; that an individual can experience 'cosmic consciousness'; and that the universe is alive, consciousness and spirit being diffused everywhere.[15]

The awareness of the Earth as a living being is not new. Indeed, it forms the basis of the 'Old Religion' – the philosophy, in its many strands and varying traditions, of the ancient people of all parts of the Earth. This is paganism, the main principles of which include an awareness of the hidden dimensions of the landscape, personified by the gods and goddesses of ancient times.

Awareness leads to knowledge and thus naturally to respect for the Earth and all living beings. In paganism there is an emphasis on those qualities which in our modern culture have been called feminine, and on co-operation with the rhythms and breath of the Earth rather than on exploiting the planet and competing with each other.

PERSON AND PLANET

By focusing on our relationship with the subtle body of the Earth, we naturally find ourselves taking on certain attitudes towards the Earth and the way we live our lives. Modern society is part of the Earth but acts as if it wasn't: ecological problems are the result. There is very little awareness of being part of the Earth, particularly among those who follow what Joseph Campbell calls 'Type II' religions, in which astrologer Robert Hand includes mechanist-materialist science.[60] If Earth Mysteries is about anything, it must be about seeking to become aware of and re-establishing these connections with the Earth at a deep level.

Healing has been mentioned throughout this book, with respect to such diverse areas as the folklore of stones, wells with curative properties, acupuncture and Reich's orgone therapy. Healing is about allowing natural energies to flow freely and thus restore balance. For example, many of those involved with Earth Mysteries testify to the curative effect of visiting ancient sites. At a more fundamental level, what is happening is that we are allowing the energy of the living Earth

to flow through us, helped by where we go and what we do. Essentially, this is a two-way process: as we become more healthy so the decisions we make which affect the Earth will be based on deeper considerations. The life force of Gaia flows through us and we realise that we are a part of her.

So, in contrast to the trend of recent generations and the whole emphasis of modern society, but in common with the ecological movement, we are led back to the landscape, and the importance of keeping its subtle detail. Earth energies may provide a guide to and underlie the essence of the health and well-being of the Earth, in the same way that the energy flows and balance in the human body are vital for the health and well-being of the person. Paul Devereux has described ecology without geomancy as being like body without soul,[28] and certainly there is a need to see and understand landscape as Watkins and more ancient peoples did – with oneself as part of it. We are part of Gaia, not separate from her, and our past and future are bound up with her. We must therefore find again her secret places, visit and respect them.

THE SIGNIFICANCE OF PLACE

Earth Mysteries affirms the significance of place. In doing so, it ranges itself against the trend of modern society, which has done so much to destroy the distinctive character of places, creating, in Nigel Pennick's telling phrase, a 'desacralized cosmos'.

To become involved in Earth Mysteries is to explore the countryside and rediscover the lost stones, paths and wells, becoming aware of the subtleness and sanctity of an area's geography. As we being to appreciate lost details and distinctions, each place begins to take an added significance, and we become able to know and to recognise the Earth in all her variety.

Time also becomes more significant as our attention is drawn towards the cycles of

Nature and the deeper, hidden cycles of the earth spirit. We come to a natural astrology, based on experience of the changing climate of being, as reflected in the changing heavens.

BELOW *Our aim is to find that integration between the Heavens and the Earth, as symbolised by the rainbow.*

CONSCIOUSNESS

Our main difficulty in understanding what was going on in prehistoric times is essentially a matter of types of consciousness. Devereux considers consciousness to be a field effect, like that around a magnet which can make iron filings fall into a pattern. Yet scientists admit to knowing virtually nothing about fields. Like Sheldrake's morphogenetic fields, they seem to underlie, and be more fundamental than, matter.

Devereux makes the point that not only were some of the ancient sites constructed by people with different purposes from us but by people in different states of consciousness from those of us now looking at the sites: the prehistoric state of consciousness is, by definition, different from the historic one. He likens it to the waking mind trying to recover dreams, the content of the unconscious mind.[28]

He believes that many sacred sites were used in altered states of consciousness produced in various ways and that, unless we understand the nature of consciousness and the nature of altered states, it is not possible fully to understand the sites. Shamanism, in all its manifestations, is crucial here as it links both consciousness and ancient sites. He says:

Until the findings of consciousness studies, now moving on apace, are brought into the matter, the question of an actual conscious, sentient planet cannot be fully dealt with. The nature of consciousness is the key. That is why consciousness studies need to become a vital component of geomantic research.[27]

THE TWO-HORSE CHARIOT

The Earth Mysteries approach is a holistic one and thus one which aims to show the links between subject areas which, to those tied to the culture of division and classification, have no apparent connection.

It is also one which requires the use of the whole brain. Brain research has shown that, generally speaking, the right side of the brain is used for intuitive types of activity, and the left side is used for intellectual matters. Techniques such as biofeedback show that, for most of use, the two halves are used disproportionately. Certainly, in our modern society, left-brain thinking is praised and encouraged, whereas right-brain activity is repressed. Both sides of the brain however must be used to experience fully sacred sites and understand ancient peoples' approach to them.

Devereux has likened the human mind to a chariot pulled by two horses: the left and right brains. If one pulls more strongly than the other, the chariot goes round in circles. In order for the mind to go anywhere, both sides

LEFT *The integration of both sides of the brain which occurs in meditation is vital for a more complete vision.*

of the brain have to be pulling evenly.[23] This integration of the analytical and the intuitive – both working together to provide a fuller and more complete vision – is not only of significance for Earth Mysteries activity: it is vital for the very survival of this planet. Earth Mysteries, by virtue of its subject matter and its approach, may be able to provide the vision and the inspiration that is so sorely needed at this time.

This need for balance has been expressed for thousands of years in China by the concept of *yin* and *yang*, where opposites are contained within the same thing which can only be considered complete if both sides are recognized. Earth Mysteries has an active and passive side, including both scientific monitoring and what Devereux has called 'being and seeing'. Both are valid approaches, the first being more *yang* and the second more *yin*.

OUTER AND INNER LANDSCAPES

My aim in writing this book has been to reveal a theme running through the wide variety of topics that go under the name of Earth Mysteries. The heart of Earth Mysteries remains our relationship to the landscape in which we live. Not just the visible landscape, but the subtle mysterious landscape which reveals itself only when we enter a state of being that can see it. It is a landscape that is inhabited by living beings, where every rock and tree and spring has significance and where we are conscious that we are part of it, part of the whole.

This is both a journey back in time, to feel again what our ancestors felt, and a journey in the present, a journey into the land. It is probably one of the most vital things that we can be called upon to do, to reintegrate with the landscape at all levels, and it is a task in which Earth Mysteries has an important role to play.

While it does have a literature that needs reading in order to avoid 'reinventing the wheel', Earth Mysteries is no old and venerated subject, hidebound by orthodoxy. It is still at the stage where it reflects the interests of those involved in it. Individuals can make a valuable contribution by exploring their local area, rediscovering ancient sites, unearthing legends from library shelves and talking to local people who still have much knowledge and wisdom to give.

As time passes, you will find yourself able to make a closer contact with the Earth by following the various ways suggested in this book. You can learn directly from the Earth herself if you approach her in the right way.

If we can learn to live according to the rhythms of the earth spirit, we will be able to integrate the different aspects of our life and recognize that we are truly part of her whole being. If there is one thing that Earth Mysteries can give, it is that awareness.

BELOW *Avebury, Wiltshire, now recognized as the centre of a symbolic landscape inhabited by people who lived according to the rhythms of the earth spirit.*

BIBLIOGRAPHY

1. ADDEY, J.M. *Harmonics in Astrology*, Fowler, 1976.
2. APPLETON, J.H. *The Experience of Landscape*, Wiley, 1975.
3. BAIGENT, M. CAMPION N. AND HARVEY, C. *Mundane Astrology*, Aquarian, 1984.
4. BENTINE, M. *The Door Marked Summer*, Granada, 1981.
5. BENTOV, I. *Stalking the Wild Pendulum*, Wildwood House, 1978.
6. BILLINGSLEY, J. 'Anarchaeology', in *Northern Earth Mysteries No.9*, October, 1980.
7. BLACK, W.H. Selected Works, Institute of Geomantic Research, 1976.
8. BLEAKLEY, A. talk to *The Ley Hunter Moot*, 1983.
9. BLIGH BOND, F. *The Gate of Remembrance*, Blackwell, 1918.
10. BOADELLA, D. *Wilhelm Reich: The Evolution of His Work*, Vision, 1973.
11. BORD, J. AND C. *The Secret Country*, Elek, 1976.
12. BRENNAN, M. *The Boyne Valley Vision*, Dolmen, 1980.
13. BROOKER, C. 'Magnetism and the Standing Stones', in New Scientist, 13 January 1983.
14. CAINE, M. *The Kingston Zodiac*, Grael, 1978.
15. CAMPBELL, J. *The Masks of God* (4 volumes), Penguin, 1976.
16. CASTLE, C. 'Megaliths in the Senegambia', in The Ley Hunter No.85, 1979.
17. COLE, T. 'One of the Durham Zodiacs', in The Ley Hunter No.14, December 1970.
18. COOPER, J. *The Case of the Cottingley Fairies*, Hale, 1990.
19. COOPER, J.C. *An Illustrated Encyclopaedia of Traditional Symbols*, Thames and Hudson, 1978.
20. COZZI, S. *Planets in Locality*, Llewellyn, 1988.
21. CUNNINGHAM, S. *Magical Aromatherapy*, Llewellyn, 1989.
22. DE BONO, E. *Practical Thinking*, Jonathan Cape, 1971.
23. DEVEREUX, P. *Earth Lights*, Turnstone, 1982.
24. - *Earthmind*, Harper and Row, 1989.
25. - *Earth Lights Revelation*, Blandford, 1989.
26. - *Places of Power*, Blandford, 1990.
27. - review in *The Ley Hunter* No. 112 Spring 1990.
28. - personal communication to the author.
29. - 'Sacred Site Dreaming', in The Ley Hunter No. 116, 1992.
30. - 'When is a Ley Not a Ley?', in The Ley Hunter No. 119, 1993.
31. - 'Dreaming On', in The Ley Hunter No. 121, Summer 1994.
32. - *Shamanism and the Mystery Lines*, Quantum, 1992.
33. - *Symbolic Landscapes*, Gothic Image, 1992.
34. - *The New Ley Hunter's Guide*, Gothic Image, 1994.
35. - and THOMSON, I. *The Ley Hunter's Companion*, Thames and Hudson, 1979.
36. - and YORK, A. 'Portrait of a Fault Area', in The News, Nos. 11 and 12, 1975.
37. DICKINSON, R. 'Kirton Lindsey, *Holy Wells*', in Markstone No. 3, Summer 1990.
38. - 'Lud's Well, Stainton-le-Vale', in Markstone No. 3, Summer 1990.
39. - 'Sacred Resonance', in Markstone No.4, Samhain 1990.
40. - 'Sounding the Landscape', in Markstone No.4, Samhain 1990.
41. DUKE, E. *The Druidical Temples of the County of Wilts*, 1846.
42. EDWARDS, L. 'The Welsh Temple of the Zodiac', in Research vol 1 no.2, July/August 1948.
43. EITEL, E.J. *Feng Shui*, Trübner, 1873.
44. FIDLER, J.H. *Ley Lines – Their Nature and Properties*, Turnstone, 1983.
45. FINDHORN COMMUNITY, *The Findhorn Garden*, Turnstone/Wildwood House, 1976.
46. FORREST, R. and BEHREND, M. *The Coldrum Ley: Chance or Design?* Forrest, 1986.
47. FORTUNE, D. *The Goat-Foot God*, William and Norgate, 1936.
48. - *The Sea Priestess*, Aquarian, 1957.
49. FRAZER, J.G. *The Golden Bough*, Macmillan, 1922.
50. FUCHS, R.H. *Richard Long*, Thames and Hudson, 1986.
51. GADSBY P. AND HUTTON-SQUIRE, C. 'A Computer Study of Megalithic Alignments', in Undercurrents No.17, Aug-Sept 1976.
52. GEALL, D. *London's Terrestrial Zodiac*, (privately published).
53. GODDARD, J. 'Earth Energy: Ten Years' Study', in Northern Earth Mysteries No.10, Winter Solstice 1980.
54. GRAVES, R. *The White Goddess*, Faber and Faber, 1952.
55. GRAVES, T. *Needles of Stone*, Turnstone, 1978.
56. - *Towards a Magical Technology*, Gateway, 1986.
57. - and J. Hoult (eds), *The Essential T.C. Lethbridge*, Routledge and Kegan Paul, 1980.
58. GREEN, M. *A Harvest of Festivals*, Longman, 1980.
59. GRINSELL, L.V. *Folklore of Prehistoric Sites in Britain*, David and Charles, 1976.
60. HAND, R. 'Astrology as a Revolutionary Science', in A.T. Mann (ed.), *The Future of Astrology*, Unwin Hyman, 1987.
61. HARTE, J. 'Haunted Roads', in The Ley Hunter No. 121, Summer 1994.
62. HAWKINS, G.S. *Stonehenge Decoded*, Souvenir, 1966.
63. HESELTON, P. *The Holderness Zodiac*, Hull, 1977.
64. - 'A Morphological Approach to the Study of Terrestrial Zodiacs', in Ancient Mysteries No. 17, Winter 1980.
65. - 'Landscape Energy and Experience', in Northern Earth Mysteries No.10, Winter Solstice 1980.
66. - 'Experiencing the Subtle Geography of the Earth'. in Northern Earth Mysteries Nos 16 and 18, February and July 1982.
67. - 'Tony Wedd: New Age Pioneer', Northern Earth Mysteries, 1986.
68. - J. GODDARD AND P. BAINES, 'Skyways and Landmarks Revisited', Northern Earth Mysteries/Surrey Earth Mysteries 1985.
69. HITCHING, F. *Earth Magic*, Cassell, 1976.
70. HODSON, G. *Fairies at Work and at Play*, Theosophical Publishing House, 1925.
71. HOWARD, M. *Earth Mysteries*, Hale, 1990.

BIBLIOGRAPHY

72. JACKSON, N.A. *The Call of the Horned Piper*, Capall Bann, 1994.

73. KILNER, W.J. *The Human Atmosphere*, Kegan Paul, 1911.

74. KIMMIS, J. *'The King's Highway'*, in The Ley Hunter No.89, 1980.

75. KOOP, K.H. *The Earliest Survey*, Research Centre, 1945.

76. LACEY B. AND BRUCE, J. *Journey round the Glastonbury Zodiac*, Lacey and Bruce, 1978.

77. LARKMAN, B. *'Walbiri Ways of Seeing'*, in Northern Earth Mysteries No.4, February 1980.

78. - *'The York Ley'*, in The Ley Hunter No. 100, Winter/Spring 1986.

79. - personal communication to the author.

80. - and HESELTON, P. *Earth Mysteries: An Exploratory Introduction*, Northern Earth Mysteries, 1985.

81. LAWTON, A. *Mysteries of Ancient Man*, 1938, republished-Paul Screeton, 1971.

82. LEVY-BRUHL, L. *Primitive Mythology*, University of Queensland Press, 1983.

83. LOCKYER, N. *Stonehenge and Other British Monuments Astronomically Considered*, Macmillan, 1906.

84. LONEGREN, S. *Spiritual Dowsing*, Gothic Image, 1986.

85. LOVELOCK, J. *Gaia: A New Look at Life on Earth*, Oxford University Press, 1979.

86. MACKIE, E.W. *Science and Society in Prehistoric Britain*, Elek, 1977.

87. MACLEAN, D. *To Hear the Angels Sing*, Findhorn, 1980.

88. MAGIN, U. *'The Christianisation of Pagan Landscapes'*, in The Ley Hunter No. 116, 1992.

89. MALTWOOD, K. *A Guide to Glastonbury's Temple of the Stars*, James Clarke, 1964.

90. MAXWELL, D. *A Detective in Surrey*, The Bodley Head, 1932.

91. MICHELL, J. *City of Revelation*, Garnstone Press, 1972.

92. - *The Old Stones of Land's End*, Garnstone Press, 1974.

93. - *The Earth Spirit*, Thames and Hudson, 1975.

94. - *A Little History of Astro-archaeology*, Thames and Hudson, 1977.

95. MILNE, A.A. *The House at Pooh Corner*, Methuen, 1928.

96. MIROV N.T. AND HASBROUCK, J. *The Story of Pines*, Indiana University Press, 1976.

97. MORRISON, T. *Pathways to the Gods*, Michael Russell, 1978.

98. MURRAY, M. *The God of the Witches*, Sampson Low, 1931.

99. NADDAIR, K. *talk to Northern Earth Mysteries Moot*, 1990.

100. NICHOLSON, J. *Folk Lore of East Yorkshire*, 1890.

101. PENNICK, N. *Nuthampstead Zodiac*, Th'Endsville, 1972.

102. - *The Mysteries of King's College Chapel*, Thorsons, 1978.

103. - (ed), *British Geomantic Pioneers 1570-1932*, Institute of Geomantic Research, 1982.

104. - *Practical Magic in the Northern Tradition*, Aquarian, 1989.

105. - and DEVEREUX, P. *Lines on the Landscape*, Hale, 1989.

106. PERRIN, J. *'Interview with John Gill'*, in High No.43, June 1986.

107. RAGLAND PHILLIPS, G. *Brigantia*, Routledge and Kegan Paul, 1976.

108. - *The Unpolluted God*, Northern Lights, 1987.

109. REEDER, P. personal communication to the author.

110. REICHENBACH, K. VON *The Mysterious Odic Force*, Aquarian, 1977.

111. ROBINS, D. *Circles of Silence*, Souvenir, 1985.

112. RUDKIN, E.H. *Lincolnshire Folklore*, Beltons, 1936.

113. RUSSELL, G.W. (AE) *The Candle of Vision*, Macmillan, 1918.

114. SCREETON, P. *'Mysterious Energies'*, in Undercurrents No. 11, May-June 1975.

115. - *The Lambton Worm and other Northumbrian Dragon Legends*, Zodiac House, 1978.

116. SHELDRAKE, R. *A New Science of Life*, Blond and Briggs, 1981.

117. SKINNER, S. *The Living Earth Manual of Feng Shui*, Routledge and Kegan Paul, 1982.

118. SMITH, R.A. *'Archaeological Dowsing'*, in Journal of the British Society of Dowsers III, June 1939.

119. SMITH, W. *Ancient Springs and Streams of the East Riding of Yorkshire*, Browns, 1923.

120. TAYLOR, I. *The All Saints' Ley Hunt*, Northern Lights, 1986.

121. - *The Giant of Penhill*, Northern Lights, 1987.

122. THOM, A. *Megalithic Sites in Britain*, Oxford University Press, 1967.

123. TREVELYAN, G. *The Active Eye in Architecture*, Wrekin Trust, 1977.

124. TRUBSHAW, R. *'Are Earth Mysteries Art?'*, in Markstone No. 4, Samhain 1990.

125. TYLER, F.C. *The Geometrical Arrangement of Ancient Sites*, Simpkin Marshall, 1939.

126. UNDERWOOD, G. *The Pattern of the Past*, Museum Press, 1969.

127. WATKINS, ALFRED *Early British Trackways*, Simpkin Marshall, 1922.

128. - *The Old Straight Track*, Methuen 1925.

129. - *The Ley Hunter's Manual*, Simpkin Marshall, 1927.

130. WATKINS, ALLEN *'My First Ley Hunt'*, in The Ley Hunter Vol 1 No. 3, 1965.

131. - *'The Straight Path in Wisdom Teaching'*, in The Ley Hunter, No. 18, 1971.

132. -Alfred Watkins of Hereford, Garnstone Press, 1972.

133. WATTS, A. *The Book on The Taboo Against Knowing Who You Are*, Jonathan Cape, 1969.

134. WEDD, J.A.D. *Skyways and Landmarks*, The STAR Fellowship, 1961.

135. - *'The Path'*, in The Ley Hunter No. 5, March 1970.

136 - *'Allotechnology: The science that got here first'*, in The Ley Hunter No.7, May 1970.

137. WEEKS, N. *The Medical Discoveries of Edward Bach, Physician*, C.W. Daniel, 1940.

138. WESTLAKE, A. *The Pattern of Health*, Stuart, 1961.

139. WHEATON, J. *'The Meridians of Man,'* in The Ley Hunter No. 11, 1970.

140. WHELAN E. AND TAYLOR, I. *Yorkshire Holy Wells and Sacred Springs*, Northern Lights, 1989.

141. WILDMAN, S. *'The Age of the Glastonbury Zodiac'*, in Terrestrial Zodiacs Newsletter No.6, May 1979.

GLOSSARY

ACUPUNCTURE The cure of disease through stimulation, by the use of needles, of specific points in the human body on the meridians, or flows of subtle energy.

ALLOTECHNOLOGY An alternative technology, using the principles of 'free energy'.

ARCHETYPES Fundamental principles of existence, part of the 'collective unconscious', which manifest in our dreams and waking life.

AURA The field of subtle energy around a living being, which can be seen by sensitives.

AUTOMATIC WRITING The ability of some sensitives to write in response to impulses originating other than in the conscious mind.

AVENUE A double line of standing stones.

BARROW A mound of earth, which may be a variety of shapes, often over a chamber.

BIOFEEDBACK Observation and manipulation of the distinctive types of brain-wave patterns accompanying the various states of consciousness, as displayed on an electro-encephalograph (EEG).

CAIRN A mound in the landscape, particularly one made of stones.

CERIDWEN Welsh moon goddess, whose cauldron gave knowledge and inspiration.

CHAKRAS Energy centres linking the subtler bodies with the physical. From the Sanskrit for 'wheels'.

CH'I The Chinese name for subtle energies in the landscape and the human body.

CIST A box made of stone slabs.

CONE OF POWER Energy built up by witches working within a magic circle.

CROMLECH A megalithic chamber, sometimes originally within a mound.

AURA

CUP AND RING MARKS Rock Carvings, perhaps dating from the Bronze Age, in the form of depressions and concentric rings.

CURSUS A linear landscape feature, dating from neolithic times.

DEVA A Sanskrit word meaning 'shining one': now applied to the archetypal formative energy-being of a particular species or overlighting a geographical area.

DOLMEN A megalithic chamber, sometimes originally within a mound.

DOWSING A means of detecting otherwise imperceptible objects or subtle energies by the movement of a rod or pendulum held in the hand.

DRAGON PROJECT An ongoing series of projects undertaken by researchers from a variety of disciplines brought together by *The Ley Hunter* magazine in an attempt to identify earth energy.

EARTH LIGHTS Visible electromagnetic discharges from the earth, especially near fault lines at times of tectonic disturbance, possibly related to ball lightning.

ELEMENTAL A nature spirit having the character of one of the elements. Also, a created thought-form.

ELEMENTS Fire, earth, air and water – basic attributes of existence to which everything can be ascribed. Sometimes an integrating fifth element, ether, is added.

EPHEMERIDES Tables used by astrologers, giving planetary positions and other data.

ETHER A fifth element, thought to permeate all space.

FENG SHUI A Chinese system which recognizes energy flows and forms in the landscape. It includes methods of modifying these forms to ameliorate the 'energy climate' of a site.

CHI'I

FIELD An area in space, usually around an object, in which certain events connected with the object take place. No physical explanation has yet been demonstrated.

FOGOU Cornish underground artificial chamber.

FREE ENERGY The name used by Tony Wedd for unknown earth and cosmic energies which could power certain devices.

GAIA The Greek earth goddess, utilized in more recent times by Dr James Lovelock to describe the entire biosystem of our planet which seems to have the ability to maintain optimum conditions for the survival of life.

GEOMANCY The science of putting human habitats and activities into harmony with the visible and invisible world around us.

HARMONIC ASTROLOGY A branch of astrology, developed by John Addey, based on the division of the aspect, zodiac and mundane circles by whole numbers.

HENGE A circular ditch and bank, where the ditch is inside the bank: for ritual rather than defense.

HEXAGRAM A six-pointed star, formed by two equilateral triangles, signifying the principle of 'as above, so below'.

HOLISTIC Coming from the same root as 'holy' and 'health', the holistic approach implies an acceptance that we are all one with the whole of existence.

HEXAGRAM

KIVA Native American ceremonial chamber.

LABYRINTHS Geometrical patterns, often of intricate design, where a single (or 'unicursal') path leads from the outside to the centre. They are found throughout Europe and may have had some ritual or meditative function.

LANDSCAPE GEOMETRY The use of sacred measure and proportion in the laying out of large-scale patterns on the surface of the Earth, including such features as leys, circles and geomantic corridors.

LABYRINTH

LEYS Alignments of ancient sites. First named by Alfred Watkins, who discovered them in 1921, although alignments had been noticed earlier by others.

LONG BARROW Neolithic mound, sometimes containing a burial.

MACROCOSM The whole universe.

LEY

MAGIC 'The Science and Art of causing change to occur in conformity with Will', according to Aleister Crowley.

MANA The subtle energy manifest in the human body, according to the Kahunas of Hawaii.

MAZES see Labyrinths.

MEGALITHS Large stones, or monuments built of them.

MENHIR A standing stone.

METROLOGY The study of measures and measurement; in Earth Mysteries especially the sacred dimensions used to measure out stone circles, cathedrals and other sacred sites.

MICROCOSM The manifestation, particularly in the human being, of particular aspects of the Macrocosm, according to the Hermetic principle of 'as above, so below'.

MORPHOGENESIS Literally, the evolution of the shape of things. Rupert Sheldrake suggests that the form, development and behaviour of living organisms are all shaped by morphogenetic fields of a type not yet recognized by science.

MULTICURSAL Having a choice of paths. Usually used of a maze or labyrinth.

NEOLITHIC The latter part of the Stone Age: the period when most megaliths were constructed.

NUMEROLOGY The study of numbers and their interrelationship, with particular emphasis on the mystical properties of particular numbers.

NWYVRE A druid name for earth energy.

OD, ODIC FORCE, ODYLE Used interchangeably by Baron Karl von Reichenbach as names for the subtle energy which he discovered.

OMPHALOS The central point, often a stone, around which a settlement develops.

OND The name for subtle energy in the Northern Tradition.

ORGONE The name given to the subtle energy discovered by Wilhelm Reich which permeates all

WILHELM REICH

living things and which has been known by a variety of names throughout history.

PAGANISM The religions of Nature, particularly where the Earth is seen and experienced as a living being, such as in witchcraft.

PENTAGRAM A five-pointed star.

PRANA The Sanskrit name for subtle energy.

PSYCHIC ARCHAEOLOGY The use of psychic means to determine information which is no longer directly available to us about some place and/or time.

PSYCHOMETRY The discovery of information about an object or its owner by holding it, or of a place by visiting it, and 'visualizing' its history.

ROUND BARROW A Bronze Age burial mound.

SACRED GEOMETRY Geometry expressed within the fabric of some architectural structure so as to cause the structure to 'resonate' when permeated by earth energies, thus affecting those people within, especially if they are attuned or sensitive to it.

DRUID

SHAMAN A person who is able to see into the subtler realms, or inner planes, by the use of various techniques, and who is able to travel in spirit in those realms for purposes such as healing.

TELLURIC FORCE A term, largely used by dowsers, for earth energy.

TERRESTRIAL ZODIACS Patterns in the landscape, often several miles across, in the form of figures of the zodiac. Thought variously to have been created in prehistoric or medieval times, the first zodiac was discovered at Glastonbury by Katherine Maltwood in the 1920s.

TUMULUS A mound, usually Bronze Age.

UNICURSAL Having only one path. Usually used of mazes and labyrinths.

VESICA PISCIS The shape formed by two intersecting circles.

WITCHCRAFT One of the main strands of paganism at the present day, possibly surviving as an unbroken link from the religion of prehistoric times. With its emphasis on special places and

YIN/YANG

WITCHCRAFT

the use of natural forces and energies, it ties in closely with Earth Mysteries.

WOUIVRE see Nwyvre.

YIN/YANG The representation of the first split into duality of the oneness of the Tao, from whence everything comes, according to Taoist philosophy. All aspects of the universe, both physical and subtle, necessarily contain and can be contrasted with, an element of its opposite.

FURTHER READING

There is now a large and growing number of books on Earth Mysteries themes. The following is merely my personal selection. It includes a few which, whilst out of print at present, are well worth seeking out in second-hand bookshops and which should be obtainable through libraries.

GENERAL

Paul Devereux, **EARTH MEMORY**, *Quantum, 1991.* A major up-to-date exposition of the whole field by the current editor of The Ley Hunter, with a strong emphasis on the structure underlying the whole subject area.
Paul Devereux, **SYMBOLIC LANDSCAPES**, *Gothic Image, 1992.* Using the case-study of the Avebury area, this book greatly advances our understanding of the significance which landscapes had for ancient peoples.
Michael Howard, **EARTH MYSTERIES**, *Hale, 1990.* An introduction to specific topics, such as astro-archaeology, hill figures, zodiacs and pyramids.
John Michell, **THE NEW VIEW OVER ATLANTIS**, *Thames and Hudson, 1983.* Michell's book The View Over Atlantis, first published in 1969, did much to spark off the current interest in Earth Mysteries. Now revised, with much new material, it concentrates particularly on numerology and sacred geometry.

ARCHAEO-ASTRONOMY

John Michell, **A LITTLE HISTORY OF ASTRO-ARCHAEOLOGY**, *Thames and Hudson, 1977.* A concise and well-illustrated summary.

DOWSING

Tom Graves, **THE ELEMENTS OF PENDULUM DOWSING**, *Element Books, 1989.* A good practical guide.
Sig Lonegren, **SPIRITUAL DOWSING**, *Gothic Image, 1986.* A good introduction on how to dowse, with an emphasis on earth energies and healing.
Guy Underwood, **THE PATTERN OF THE PAST**, *Museum Press, 1969.* A classic text, giving full details of the author's methods and findings.

EARTH ENERGIES

Paul Devereux, **EARTH LIGHTS**, *Turnstone, 1982, and* **EARTH LIGHTS REVELATION**, *Blandford, 1989.* These concentrate particularly on reports of UFOs and show a link to tectonic activity within the earth and to stone circles. A wealth of new and fascinating material is included.
Paul Devereux, **PLACES OF POWER**, *Blandford, 1990.* The subtitle is 'Secret Energies at Ancient Sites: A Guide to Observed or Measured Phenomena'. It is an account of the work of the Dragon Project and associated findings at Rollright and other ancient sites throughout Britain.
Tom Graves, **NEEDLES OF STONE REVISITED**, *Gothic Image, 1986.* A practical and speculative book on earth energies, including earth acupuncture, feng shui and paganism.
John Michell, **THE EARTH SPIRIT**, *Thames and Hudson, 1975.* A brilliant essay on earth energies to accompany a book of remarkable photographs.

FOLKLORE

Janet and Colin Bord, **THE SECRET COUNTRY**, *Paul Elek 1976.* This is an excellent account of legends associated with particular sites, from all over the British Isles. The Bords classify these by type, and show how they might be explained in terms of earth energies.
Leslie V Grinsell, **FOLKLORE OF PREHISTORIC SITES IN BRITAIN**, *David and Charles, 1976.* An authoritative account of the various motifs which appear in folklore, together with a good gazetteer of ancient sites and their associated legends.

SACRED GEOMETRY

Nigel Pennick, **SACRED GEOMETRY**, *Capall Bann, 1995.* Subtitled 'Symbolism and Purpose in Religious Structures', this book takes a chronological approach to the various forms of sacred geometry.

HOLY WELLS

Janet and Colin Bord, **SACRED WATERS – HOLY WELLS AND WATER LORE IN BRITAIN AND IRELAND**, *Granada, 1985.* Includes a gazetteer of 200 holy wells.

LEYS

Paul Devereux, **THE NEW LEY HUNTER'S GUIDE**, *Gothic Image, 1994.* A new and updated version of the 1979 book, *The Ley Hunter's Companion*, this is a practical handbook and field guide giving full instructions on how to go about finding leys.
Paul Devereux, **SHAMANISM AND THE MYSTERY LINES**, *Quantum, 1992.* Probably the most important book on leys in recent years, it shows that they are, in essence, spirit lines, originating in the straight magical flight of the shamans.
Nigel Pennick and Paul Devereux, **LINES ON THE LANDSCAPE – LEYS AND OTHER LINEAR ENIGMAS**, *Hale, 1989.* This brings the story of leys up to date, with information on linearity in the landscape throughout the world.
Alfred Watkins, **THE OLD STRAIGHT TRACK**, *Methuen, 1925; reprinted Garnstone 1970.* This is the classic text on leys, describing Watkins' discoveries and theories, well illustrated with examples of leys and mark points, mainly in his native Herefordshire, and with his remarkable photographs.

MAZES AND LABYRINTHS

Nigel Pennick, **MAZES AND LABYRINTHS**, *Hale, 1990.* A thorough study of labyrinths throughout the world and their development. Includes a useful gazetteer of existing mazes.

SACRED SITES

Marian Green, **THE ELEMENTS OF NATURAL MAGIC**, *Element Books, 1989.* An excellent, and wise, guide from one who knows what she is writing about. All Marian Green's books are good.

Most Earth Mysteries books should be readily obtainable from alternative and occult bookshops. A particularly wide range is stocked by:
The Atlantis Bookshop, 49a Museum Street, London WC1A 1LY
Compendium, 234 Camden High Street, London NW1 8QS
Gothic Image, 7 High Street, Glastonbury, Somerset BA6 9DP
A mail order service is operated by Empress Ltd, PO Box 92, Penzance, Cornwall TR18 2XL.

USEFUL INFORMATION

USEFUL ADDRESSES

One of the ways to keep in touch with current Earth Mysteries activities is to subscribe to the various magazines devoted to the subject, all of which are produced on an amateur basis and which need support.

It is inevitable that information on such magazines very quickly becomes out of date, particularly details of subscription rates, which are therefore not given.

The Ley Hunter, PO Box 92, Penzance, Cornwall TR18 2XL. The longest-running Earth Mysteries journal in the world, and still the foremost in its field.

Northern Earth, John Billingsley, 10 Jubilee Street, Mytholmroyd, Hebden Bridge, West Yorkshire HX7 5NP.

Markstone (Journal of the Lincolnshire and East Yorkshire Earth Mysteries Group), Jane and Bob Dickinson and Philip Heselton, Glebe Farm House, Fen Road, Owmby-by-Spital, Lincoln LN2 3DR.

Touchstone (Journal of the Surrey Earth Mysteries Group), Jimmy Goddard, 25 Albert Road, Addlestone, Surrey KT15 2PX.

Meyn Mamvro (Cornish Earth Mysteries), Cheryl Straffon, 51 Carn Bosavern, St Just, Penzance, Cornwall TR19 7QX.

Mercian Mysteries, Bob Trubshaw, 2 Cross Hill Close, Wymeswold, Loughborough, Leicestershire LE12 6UJ.

Third Stone, PO Box 258, Cheltenham, Gloucestershire GL53 0HR.

Wisht Maen (Devon Earth Mysteries), Condors, Exeter Street, North Tawton, Devon EX20 2HB.

New England Antiquities Research Association Journal, 2 Oxford Place, Worcester MA 01609 USA.

The other way of getting to know what is going on in the Earth Mysteries field is to attend one of the gatherings (often called 'Moots') which are held from time to time. The main Moot is that organized by *The Ley Hunter* magazine, which has been held annually in different parts of the country since 1977. Other groups, including the Northern Earth Mysteries Group, also hold an annual Moot, together with smaller gatherings, often going out into the countryside to visit a site or follow a ley that someone knows. Details can be obtained from the respective editors.

Most Earth Mysteries activity seems to be centred around regional and local Earth Mysteries magazines, and there are specific organizations corresponding to many of the magazines. Other organizations include the Research into Lost Knowledge Organisation (RILKO), 8 The Drive, New Southgate, London N11 2DY and The London Earth Mysteries Circle, PO Box 1035, London W2 6ZX.

Mention must also be made of the Dragon Project Trust, which received charitable status in 1987 and which was created to continue and develop the work of the Dragon Project. It is also studying the effects on consciousness at sites where specific geophysical anomalies have been noted (see Chapter 5). The Trust is the only organization attempting research into measurable or observable energy effects at ancient sites and, without funds, the Project will die. Donations of money, work and skills will be gratefully received by the Trust, c/o Empress, PO Box 92, Penzance, Cornwall TR18 2XL.

ACKNOWLEDGEMENTS

Cameron Collection: 15, 86. **Fine Art Photographic Library:** 52, 73, 84, 89, 90/91B, 100, 101. **Fortean Picture Library:** 54, 66B, 69T; **Klaus Aarsleff:** 53, 63, 87T; **Paul Broadhurst:** 9R, 32, 42, 45B, 50, 51, 70, 71; **Janet and Colin Bord:** 2/3, 6, 10, 18/19, 22, 25L, 26, 28, 31, 38, 39, 47, 48, 49L + R, 56/57B, 60, 67B, 68B, 74, 78, 81, 85T + B, 95, 98, 103; **James Croker:** 33; **Loren Coleman:** 35T; **Dr Elmar Gruber:** 67T, 88T; **Dr G. T. Meaden:** 23B, 77T; **Philip Panton:** 12, 16B, 29; **Gerald Ponting:** 27B; **Roger Vlitos:** 14/15; **Anthony Weir:** 64, 76. **Glasgow Museum and Art Gallery** (J. N. Paton: *The Fairy Raid* details): 8, 82T. **Philip Heselton:** 24, 55, 66, 88B, 89, 94, 96/7. **The Image Bank:** 8/9, 20, 40, 41, 77. **Images Colour Library:** 13, 16T, 17, 25BR, 35B, 37T, 58B, 75. **Stuart Littlejohn:** 36B. **Brian Larkman and Jerry Hardman-Jones:** 56TL. **Mary Evans Picture Library:** 102. **NASA:** 7T, 39C. **Science Photo Library/Oscar Burriel/Latin Stock:** 99. **South American Pictures: Tony Morrison:** 21T, 79.